A NOBODY'S NOTEBOOK

SANDEEP DAHIYA

Copyright © Sandeep Dahiya
All Rights Reserved.

This book has been self-published with all reasonable efforts taken to make the material error-free by the author. No part of this book shall be used, reproduced in any manner whatsoever without written permission from the author, except in the case of brief quotations embodied in critical articles and reviews.

The Author of this book is solely responsible and liable for its content including but not limited to the views, representations, descriptions, statements, information, opinions and references ["Content"]. The Content of this book shall not constitute or be construed or deemed to reflect the opinion or expression of the Publisher or Editor. Neither the Publisher nor Editor endorse or approve the Content of this book or guarantee the reliability, accuracy or completeness of the Content published herein and do not make any representations or warranties of any kind, express or implied, including but not limited to the implied warranties of merchantability, fitness for a particular purpose. The Publisher and Editor shall not be liable whatsoever for any errors, omissions, whether such errors or omissions result from negligence, accident, or any other cause or claims for loss or damages of any kind, including without limitation, indirect or consequential loss or damage arising out of use, inability to use, or about the reliability, accuracy or sufficiency of the information contained in this book.

Made with ♥ on the Notion Press Platform
www.notionpress.com

For Ma and Pa

Contents

Foreword	*vii*
Acknowledgements	*ix*
1. Chapter 1	1
2. Chapter 2	24
3. Chapter 3	48
4. Chapter 4	71
5. Chapter 5	93
6. Chapter 6	114
7. Chapter 7	133
8. Chapter 8	152

Foreword

These are little snippets of life in the past and the present. I stay at a village and the rural society presents its sweet-sour agrestic culturescape. One may have, especially those who have spent their lives in the cities, an idyllic idea about life in the villages. Well, things are idyllic in nature but you cannot escape the volatility presented by a conglomeration of humans, even at the scale of little hamlets.

Even though right in the middle of it, I stay at its fringes as far as participation is concerned. I live almost within the premises of my house, only coming out when the essentials of life force me out. I have my little garden and small courtyard in my old, cracking countryside house that allows me to even go for walks like a caged lion does—to and fro, to and fro; from one end to the other.

It's a small world within and a humongous one outside. Little birds, insects, flowers, plants and some small trees in my yard provide me a space, a kind of microscopic view of the larger realities outside. It serves as a little lab of experimentation with thoughts, ideas, perspectives, judgments and of course poetic dreams and imaginations. It provides a bit of stability in this shaky world. I salvage my meaning of life primarily from little happenings among these few flowerbeds and the little clump of small trees in my yard. Life comes peaceful, simple and enjoyable, a kind of little 'meaning' amidst all the puzzling realities around.

And a little secluded corner is very conducive to pamper nostalgic memories from the past. So the leisurely bait catches some memories from the swift currents of time. It's a very nice feeling to visit those times. These memories serve as an exotic spice to make the chronicles

FOREWORD

still tastier.

Of course, I peep over the walls also, driven by the natural human curiosity, to see what is going outside. The crude, easy as well as hard-going farmers lead a very loud, interesting life. It but may not fit comfortably with the sensibilities of an introvert writer. Most of the time, things are tragic and comic simultaneously. On the basis of your mood, you have the option to choose either of the two. In the current compilation, I have noted down mostly the episodes and observations that have rib-tickled me positively.

I hope these little anecdotes from my past and the present bring a little bit of sunshine in the life of my readers. If my reader gets a little smile on her lips while reading this notebook, I would take it as mission accomplished.

Sandeep Dahiya
November, 2022

Acknowledgements

In eternal gratitude to all those who still believe in goodness, love, peace and harmony for all of us!

1

Thousands of fungus gnats, tiny insects of the size of one-tenth of an inch, flew into the lighted verandah. They seemed in great spirits, almost in party mood on a special night. I find them dead in the morning. But then maybe they danced to death. There are heaps of tiny dead insects among dry yellow *neem* leaves and dead rose petals. Dying together with so many of your species must be a strange experience. I broom the floor and almost countless tiny fliers form a fistful of brown sawdust. Where did so many individual points of consciousness go?

It's a windy mid October morning shoving away the lugubrious, sleepy shades from my little garden and small courtyard. An extremely chatty purple sunbird couple sounds like an excited sparrow played in fast-forward mode on an audio tape. It builds a momentum and lots of yellow and old *neem* leaves tumble down. A very soft, light drizzle gets inspired, almost wispy brushstrokes of mist, or you can say stormy mist at the most.

Marigolds love October and are quick to give the flashiest of smiles. The bougainvillea is also doing well. It's a bonsai variety to check its rapid sprawl and the consequent overtaking of the garden walls. During its purchase, when it was a tiny sapling, the nursery guy thrice corrected me on 'bonsai'. 'It's bone-size!' he informed me emphatically. I stand corrected and call it 'bone-size'. He had earlier worked at Pune and sold it under the same name to far more important and significant looking gentlemen than me, so that acted as a validation for his name and I accepted it. So the bone-size bougainvillea is trying to break the limits imposed on its wild growth by our scientists.

In a crack in the wall, there is a sprout of common purselane. It's slightly sturdy but quite stubborn to grow even on the roofs and walls. It has yellow flowers, which later dry to thorny bulbs and give a pricking retort when you try to pull them out. We call them *bhaakri* in local parlance. I decide to be stubborn like *bhaakri* in my restful or call it idle ways. Varied life situations try to tickle at my spine with their urgent toes. I, but, sit cuddling fodder like an old, relaxed ox.

The flowerbeds in the garden give a wild look as ubiquitous weeds take a foothold. Allow, sometimes, mother nature to leave its unrestricted footprint around you. It's a peculiar medley of weedy world. The shovel, digging fork and hand trowel have lots of rust bestowed by prolonged rest. Human idleness is maybe a boon for wilderness. Mother earth won't mind too many idlers. Maybe she is wary of too hardworking and smart humans. She has amply rewarded my idlehood.

Little clumps of single-stemmed quack grass with long leaf-blades are nicely clothing earth. There is false tobacco, elephant's foot, clumps of finer grasses spread like a leafy claw, hairy crabgrass with its wispy hair or call it flowers, matted sandmat or the little ground creeper with sinewy stalk and little leaves, common groundsel with frilled leaves, horseweed with its rosette of leaves. It's a miniscule marvel, a pampered luxury, enthralling opulence, a grand interlude, a kind of slice of wilderness far away from the twittering long romps of the control freaks trapped in their own cleverness.

There is a friendly rivalry among these little denizens of the grassy world. I gape at the inexorable force of mother nature. It sprawls indescribably. Nature is always at peace while we are forever shuddering and caught in an ensnaring jiffy.

A touch of the untamed grass and distant memories rush up with aplomb and fruit jam sweetness.

Tai Surje ki bahu, the wife of uncle Surje, was a pioneer in neighborhood feminism. She smoked *beedis* and hookahs with macho voracity. She drank homemade liqueur with a proud exhortation. Novice liquor-lovers got their first lessons in the art in her patronizing company. They would sit around her on the mud floor and gloat over her bartending skills using teacups with broken handles and jarred mouths.

A full bottle got toppled one day. Almost half of its contents formed a puddle in a hollow near her feet on the mud floor. She was quick to act and gave the best lesson in the art of wining and dining. She cupped her hands and splurged the earth-scented cocktail. Her pupils followed suit. It was wiped clean.

'Every drop matters. We had forgotten to offer a ceremonial drop to mother earth, so she got angry and tried to gulp down the entire bottle. As a good drinker, never forget to offer a drop to mother earth before you start,' she told them.

She is long gone, but her pupils, in their middle age now, are the present day master liquor-lovers and carry the flag high in the art and craft of full-time intoxication.

ᐩᐩᐩ

My brother loved pets during childhood. We still remember those dogs, cats and birds. A few of them stand out. Kalu was a tiniest, skinniest puppy that was bought for fifty paisa from a neighborhood urchin by my brother. It was touted as a bad bargain by the elders as it was almost on the verge of death. It kept its neck tilted as if as a declaration of misery and sickness.

The village school was nearby and we would come during the recess more to check if Kalu was still around and less to have a hurried lunch. But Kalu was a hard life in a frail body. Mother would go to the fields to get fodder and keep it chained in a wall's shade and would return before the sun crossed over and baked it alive. Once she got late and found Kalu stretched out under a merciless sun, struggling for breaths. She thought these were death pangs. But once in the shade and some water dropped in its mouth, it made a comeback and never looked back.

Kalu wasn't an all-black dog, it was speckled black and white and we chose black from the binary scheme of its coat to name it as such. It came to be a sturdy dog in its youth. Childhood frailties don't always mean the same in youth. It was now a big dog and well behaved in manners. But it would lose its temper slightly at the sight of a farmer in the locality.

One day, in anger the farmer poked at Kalu with a hayfork. Kalu lost one of its eyes. Father worked at Delhi with Life Insurance Corporation. On his return at night, we shared the catastrophic episode. We had never seen Father leading a quarrel with his little pack. But that day he led all of us to the farmer's threshold and all of us delivered a handy condemnation and wholesale remonstration. More than Kalu losing its eye, the fact that we the educated guys went for a verbal fight made the news in the village. Kalu was nursed back to health and performed well even as a one-eyed canine. It looked very cute with its squinting look. But then one day, it followed the ladies, Mother being one of them, going to the fields. It involved a kilometer of walk along the tar road. There it met its end under a truck like most of the village dogs did during those days.

Village dogs went to the roads to die. They actually ran into the vehicles to escape from them. A few other pet dogs met the same end. Rikki but was a different sort. It was a large, handsome brown and white dog. It looked a canine rockstar from all angles. It always created a timorous creak in the hearts of all the female canines. There was an ominous fluctuation in the jealous hearts of rival males as Rikki wooed almost all the females in the entire village.

After its love episodes, it looked solemn, drowsy, almost venerable. An ineffable moonbeam lurking on its august face. Its love-sorties took it to all corners of the village to shower its dreamy gaze at all its fans. Jealousy of rival dogs knew no bounds. A dozen of them banded together and ambushed the handsome Romeo. The destiny's gale was blowing against Rikki now. It was a frightful and shadowy attack in the fields outside the village. The gusting billows of their anger poured out their immeasurable agony. We were crestfallen as it was declared dead in the attack.

Almost daily pestered by my younger brother, Father came very close to buy an eagle from old Delhi. My brother had been carefully deliberating over the menu of mice and frogs for the esteemed hunter. But then the prayers of our mother were heeded and the hunter bird didn't arrive. But many pigeons and parrots did arrive, most of whom would die and my brother would mourn the death of his pet birds with loud tears.

Once there was a pair of little Australian parrots in the house. One of them flew away one day. My brother led a frantic search operation after a nippy discussion with his pals. They led their search party across the fields surrounding the village, peeked into hundreds of trees, and shot queries about the runaway parrot at the farmers from the neighboring villages grazing their cattle.

Imagine trying to spot a little bird among thousands of birds chattering among thousands of trees across many square kilometers. But a valiant marksman is undaunted by the unfavorable winds. The relentless search operation made it a local news item. Who says efforts go waste? You always stand a chance of finding even a needle in a huge hayrack if you are diligent and persevere in your effort. Someone informed that a boy at the farther end of the village has a beautiful parrot. My brother and his band sneaked over their yard to check. There it was. Sitting on a stick with its leg tied. The boy was condemned as a wicked and impious brigand, smuggler and poacher (all together) and the bird was retrieved.

Pushed by the benevolent gaiety of childhood, we once saved two hare babies from the fields. But in reality, we had kidnapped them from their house. We customized a big wooden chest as a cage. They grew fabulously. But then they started quarrelling all day and emitted stanching white urine. They had to be given to a bigger pet lover along with the huge wooden chest, sack of feed, a few rupees and plenty of cajoling.

Given their unbecoming ways, they did rounds around the village. Finally, an enterprising one ate them. We raised a protest at this but he flatly told us, 'See, you weren't the owners. I was the owner at the time.' 'But they were pets for playing,' we tried to reason. 'For playing, yea! We tried to play with them. But they were so angry that bit the finger of my grandson. Left it bleeding! So there was no other use. Moreover, there were guests at home that day and we were drunk. So made use of them.' We demanded back our huge wooden cage contrived from a chest. But to him it belonged to the last occupant. So the question of ownership got muddled along the series comprising all the owners along the line of occupancy across the village. So we lost our claim. We tried to retrieve it by stealth. It was too big for being stolen over the wall of his yard. It crashed and Bablu, the most muscular one in the squad, got a blue toe. We had to run away to avoid a beating.

Once a cat ate mama squirrel, leaving three orphaned finger-length squirrel babies sticking on an unplastered wall. My brother used all his boyhood expertise in catching them and raised them as their single parent. A slim plastic eyedropper, having a very thin nozzle, was salvaged from the waste heap. The squirrel kids would have a semi-fluid made of milk and crushed bread. They would hold the dropper's tube with their front paws and cutely drank the nourishing drink. It was a successful rearing. They grew strong. We left them on a *neem* tree where they grew still bigger and enjoyed the sweet-sour offerings of this world.

While the village boys hit the hard cork ball to neighboring field around the school playground, my brother once hit upon the scheme to fish out three handsome, full-grown parrot lads from their hideouts in the school's roof. They were just a few days away from flying and their beaks gave him a bloodied taste on fingers. I would say it was outright kidnapping. They were force-fed for a few days and raised lots of squeaky protests in the room. Then luck smiled at them. Mother inadvertently opened the door and they had their first free flight. It amounted to a real flight to freedom.

A cat mom was once staying in our barn with her week-old kittens. Grandfather turned a cat-killer for her sake. Well, we siblings turned very fond of the kittens. But then a burly male cat came at night and broke one kitten's neck leaving us fuming for revenge. We were ready for it the next night. Father had his hockey stick and Grandpa had his well-oiled stick. Grandpa was in his late seventies at that time. The rascally cat gave a tough challenge and would have escaped over the high wall if not for Grandpa's masterstroke. He jumped in air and hit the climber on its back. The cat rolled down and after that Grandpa showed amazing skill and agility in hitting maximum strikes within the shortest time. Very soon the murderer cat got murdered itself. We were so happy but Mother was apprehensive. 'They say if you kill a cat, God will demand a golden cat from you,' she reminded us. 'For that God will have to first give me that much of gold,' Grandpa seemed ready for atonement.

Sherry the black German shepherd was Father's darling. She was the only one who understood his fabulous literary English and responded to his philosophical talks. The rest of the village was clueless to his high-standard *angrezi*. But then Sherry developed a taste for running after humans and sometimes even taste some scraps of skins on human calf muscles. Complaints arose in very exaggerated proportions. Maybe the people held a grudge against her for her English skills. Father left her with a friend who stayed at the town twelve kilometers away. I think he forgot the basic fact about the canine sense of smell. But he realized it the very next night when Sherry scraped her paws against the door, whining to be admitted in. Father thought that she must have learnt a lesson and would behave well. But

Sherry looked for revenge now. I think she understood that the entire neighborhood had conspired against her. Father tried his best to put reason in her brain in classy English. But she scaled up her pursuit of human calf muscles. Complaints swarmed when Father would come back from office at night. So away they went as co passengers in the train to the capital. Father left her in the bathroom, safely locked for a long journey. That was a sad decision but that's what he could think of as a solution.

Then there were a few little mushy cats that would sneak into our quilts and give purring, pampering sounds on cold, shivery nights. These were expert cherubs and would materialize in the dark and would look out for the most comfortable quilt. They had a lot of choice.

Once one little kitten rolled on the ground to kill a common wolf snake, a baby pink, beautifully pattered little snake. Father declared the kitten to be a hunter. He gave special instructions for this particular baby cat to be treated well. He was sure that it would turn into a majestic hunter and would wipe away all the rodents and reptiles in the village. It grew fat on that promise and ran away one fine day, pursuing a girl cat and forgot all our affection.

I, on my part, had my modest share of stealing eggs from holes and nests under a conviction that if I keep them in my custody, the baby bird coming out will be my friend for life. I kept them in alcoves and skylight ledges, repeatedly checking if my birdie friend had arrived. The eggs but remained good museum pieces. I would only realize and understand the reasons in middle school science books about hatching.

ᚠᚠᚠ

We eagerly looked forward to weddings at our village during childhood, especially the girl weddings. Cheap, various-colored sweets looked like divine desserts in those days. But then a girl's marriage would mean the groom's wedding party coming to the village. It's very difficult to decipher the entire set of monstrosities unleashed by the sloshed wedding party members. It was a special day for them under patriarchal rules. So even their most goonish conduct was viewed as funny at the most. They were entitled to the entire set of follies expected from a sloshed person.

They would mistreat the music band members, kick the groom's horse, wallow in mud, shout profanities, make lewd gestures and make passes at the entire village womenfolk. Save the groom, whose face radiated some semblance of grace for getting a wife, the rest of his party would be a perfect example of ugliness and puerilities. It was a kind of unutterable indulgence that chucked out the entire village's peace.

No wonder, thrashing the groom's party before seeing off the bride wasn't an exception. They would unleash a firmament and the helpless villagers, cumbered with fathomless woes, would forget the sublimities of welcome offered to the party a few hours ago and pounce upon the evil. It was a gigantic necessity to do so in most of the cases.

The drunk revelers would do snake and monkey dance to the drumbeats and throw coins and even 10 rupee notes in the air. It would enkindle a stampede among the onlooking village boys and they would rush to pick up the coins. Then the impervious *baratis* would beat the culprits who had picked the coins. And the beaten boys would take revenge later. As the buses and other vehicles started to go back, they would throw stones to break the maximum number of windowpanes and rival heads if possible.

Once we felt well recompensed when we hammered a wooden piece into the exhaust pipe of a wedding party bus and it won't start causing a lot of anxiety and inconvenience among the foes. This slimy novelty was hurtled in their face because one of the boys from our group had been slapped because he had caught a 10-rupee note mid air that was hurled into the skies by a wildly drunk *barati* in celebration. So the bus won't start for a long time and once it did there was a hail of stones. That's how weddings were celebrated during our childhood in the eighties of the last century.

ᛈᛈᛈ

Father started experimenting with smoking *beedies* while he was in class three. Grandfather notched up many devices with squirming moralities to teach him a lesson. Father was tied to a wall peg like a tiny bale hanging in air against the wall. He was made to sign a declaration that he would never smoke and sign it 1000 times in the presence of witnesses. He was hoisted in air and dropped multiple times on the ground as a deterrence. He was made to draw lines on earth with his nose, each time saying 'I won't smoke!' Teachers were asked to be extra punitive. While all this was being done, everyone around was smoking hookahs. So the tactics failed and Father happily continued smoking *beedies* into his seventies. We also tried smoking on Pa's leftover *beedi* stubs. But it was bitter and the thing never appealed to our taste.

ᛈᛈᛈ

Trummp arrived with greenish pomp and reddish glow on its nose. The guy had a talismanic greed. Give it anything from fresh salads to cooked *kadhai paneer*, it would sumptuously eat whatever it saw you eating. The kind intention to keep him swiftly glided into an arduous task. When we got him, we held him in high consideration. But all respect for him lay hither thither just within three weeks. My temper raised its stick with an iron-shot end. Joyous countenance scampered away. Enormous and formidable was its appetite. All this while he was riding the high and mighty horse of gluttonous enthusiasm. I helplessly let out guffaws of desperation.

Well, Trummp was a parrot. An ascetic lives in a hut by the canal outside the village among the fields. He arranged for a community feast in memory of his guru. He had invited me so I went there a bit in advance while the *prasada* we still being prepared by the cooks. The parrot was leisurely patrolling the cooking area, nicely gobbling boiled potatoes, cooked pumpkin, *puris* and *ladoos*. They tried to shoo it away but it would take a little flight and come back.

The ascetic proposed that I take it. Agreeing to the proposal, we procured a cage and it was ceremoniously carried into the house. There was lingering, delectable charm about the bird. It was fat and lazy. It had philandering appetite. Its only motto seemed to be, 'You have to give something to eat the moment you see me'. The cage tray would soon get flooded with its drops. It was pretty vocal about its eating aspirations and hungry assertiveness. It was almost paranoid about its eating habit. Deprive it of anything that you were seen eating and it would try to break the cage, the only time when it showed some physical exercise. The rest of the time, it was content to just sit on its perch and scan any opportunity to eat something.

I knew that it was a female because the red collar on the neck was missing. Still I treated it as male, in fact christened it as a male so that I could use cuss words on its person to vent out my frustration. It's imperative to maintain decorum and one shouldn't use ill words against a lady bird. So I imagined it to be a male rascal.

One day, I had put the cage under the sun so that Trummp could sunbathe and get vitamin D. A male parrot, vow what a sight with its red collar around neck, came screeching for companionship. He saw the pampered fat woman in the cage and immediately fell in love. Trummp also looked at it with a friendly regard. But it didn't look too eager for free air as if it was enjoying a kind of sad enlightenment inside the cage. The passion of the love-blinded parrot was fiery and spiraling on the other hand. My compulsions were wearing thin under the constant bombardment of its demand for more and more varieties of food.

The parrot in love returned the next day also as the lazy, fat ladylove contentedly sunned its feathers. It would have been foolish not to see it happily married and lead a happy married life. After that it would be the husband's duty to see to his wife's culinary tastes. The first choice should be to transfer the responsibilities—instead of cutting them altogether—if you find them too heavy to carry on.

I opened the cage expecting the fat woman to go flying with its lover instantly. But it won't come out. Food was dearer than any lover in the world. The lover was hovering around with measureless mirth. I had to literally prod out the lady's prodigious and imperturbable laziness. The shy bride finally came out and the groom encouraged it to take a bit of flight for conjugal bliss. I immediately shut the cage and ran away with it lest the bride got its groom into it also to make him a *ghar jamai*.

Well, sadly though, one cannot survive with a luminous conscience and radiant uprightness during the present times. Anyway, hope they had a nice married life. Moreover, a few days of freedom are better than years inside a cage.

཯཯཯

As a boy uncle Satbir had lots of issues against going to school. So much so that Grandfather would hoist him up like a fodder bundle and dumped him in the class. In his childish keenness uncle Satbir would prefer to be out of the school. That was his first choice. Grandfather was once a teacher and his injunctions about life centered around school and *mashakkat*, hard practice, on mathematics primarily. So, despite uncle Satbir's protestations, it was foreordained that he had to go to school and love mathematics.

Then some mysterious nerves tweaked in his brain and uncle Satbir grabbed the mathematical sinews in their entire minuteness. The teachers would be found to be inadequate to handle his mathematical wizardry and unrelenting queries. With a jingling enthusiasm uncle Satbir cracked the IIT entrance examination. It was a commendable feat for a village boy who loved wallowing in the pond holding the tails of buffalos. Uncle studied aeronautical engineering at IIT Kanpur. But the fleeting quotients of the mathematics of his life found it a perfidy to be stuck up in an institution. Despite doing really well in studies there, Uncle stood by his unadulterated scruples and ran away from the august institution. Grandfather got a letter from the premier engineering college that his ward had gone missing. With a sly lightness, Uncle simply vanished in thin air. Maybe he found institutions as a kind of ferocious and hideous iron collar around his neck and broke free.

After five years of absconding, my father tracked him in Yamuna Nagar. When Father reached the spot, Uncle was the undisputed king of accounting in the truck union office. Father saw him on a rickety desk, a panama hat on his head, a bottle of local liquor in front, an account book open and the mathematics wizard expertly settling the transporters' sums. It was very difficult to extricate him from the brotherly grasp of burly Sikh drivers, who thought the truck union would fall to pieces without its young, three-quarter IITian.

Back home, despite the outrageousness of his deed, he was convinced to enroll in B.Sc. degree course at the local college in the town. Uncle resplendently declared that he would top the university. And he did. Meanwhile, he made life impossible for the professors, who would fold hands and ask him to enjoy life outside because he knew all that they had to teach. Uncle walked and talked mathematics. It made Grandfather pardon all his goof-ups and sins against education.

A friend of Uncle was struggling to clear his matriculation exams. There was a chance to join police but the matriculation certificate was the roadblock. Uncle loved the idea of appearing in matriculation exams as proxy for those who won't pass even fifth class exams of their own. He got a few of them pass with first class degrees. Unfortunately, as he appeared for this friend he was caught. Uncle always thought that he did the job with an incorruptible conscience because he never took monetary remuneration for writing exams for poor students. Anyway, he was caught and a case lodged against him. He had his very own rallying points and said no to hire any lawyer to fight his case. He appeared before the judge and gave his declaration:

'Your Honor, I know I have broken the law but I have done it for a good cause. This friend of mine is very poor. He has lost his mother also. A matriculation certificate would get him a policeman's job but he cannot pass it himself. I did it for him. Had I taken money for it, I would have accepted my crime.'

Wonder of wonders, the judge let him go with a warning against repeating the same in future.

A marriage proposal came and Uncle just shook his head that meant neither 'yes' nor 'no'. In any case, they got him married without pondering over too much about the purported meaning of the shake of his head. After six months of conjugal experiment, Uncle again heard the lugubrious echo of freedom from all institutions. Amidst the engulfing tumult of protestations by his young wife, Uncle declared he cannot live with her. When Grandfather protested against this declaration, Uncle flatly countered, 'She can stay in the house but I will leave!' And he vanished like he had escaped from the clutch hold of the IIT college. He ran away. This time almost forever.

Even while on the move like a nomad, he would have many admirers involving both institutions and individuals. Mathematics wizard as he was. After a lot of escapades for freedom, he opened an IIT coaching institution at Dehradoon and raised a fantastic breed of IITians, many of whom settled abroad. He did all this with a limping leg and continuous, niggling pain.

Destiny seemed to hunt him with a grievous and fatal precision. At the age of forty, he met an accident while riding a scooter. He was dragged by an unknown vehicle and the scooter's handle tore through his stomach, exposing the whole mass of intestines. He held his organs tightly in his grasp till help came and only then fainted. At New Delhi AIIMS, critically short of staff under the onslaught of the entire country's critical cases, he lay waiting for some doctor to be free as life slowly crept out of him. Death peeked over perilous precipices. But Uncle was braced against the final fall. He called a junior doctor and told him, 'Roberts you have to do this operation. Don't worry, I am not going to die. You will simply be an instrument of my survival.' The surgery went for almost twelve hours. And as he had promised, Uncle survived.

He carried a huge line of stitch marks along his abdomen. From the same accident, he carried a leg injury that won't heal. A kind of gangrene ulcer. It was almost raw flesh around the shin. Look at it and you would shudder with horror and pain. 'The pain that would make you cry is normal for me now,' he would say. It would need multiple dressings in a day. He got accidental hernia also along the stitching in his abdomen. It protruded with a big growth but he could not be operated because of the non-healing nature of his leg injury. So Uncle had to tie himself in a belt to hold his hernia growth.

He tried all forms of medications to cure his leg and finally became an expert homeopath in search for the ever-elusive cure for his injury. He muzzled up the classic Homeopathic treatises and in fact became more knowledgeable about Homoeopathy than the professional degree holders. He kept on searching for some miraculous concoction of herbal medicines that would cure him. He always had a firm belief in a solution because mathematically every problem has a solution. This was the toughest problem that kept him busy for the last twenty-two years of his life. And carrying all this burden of physical pain, he raised a very successful IIT coaching academy that produced hundreds of IITians.

But no institution was strong enough to hold his formidable and raw sense of freedom. He made the institution and after a decade broke it himself. One of the teachers was almost like an adopted son to him. He stayed with Uncle with his very courteous and diligent wife. It was a happy family in every sense of the term. They made a huge house in the luxurious foothills of the Doon valley. The academy was doing perfectly well. They had big cars. Then one fine day, Uncle again broke loose from the shackles of normalcy. Like a child suddenly scatters the sand castle it had so laboriously erected on the beach, Uncle suddenly swiped and closed the system. He parted from the son-like teacher. He divided the assets, gave them everything and kept just the residence with him. The academy was given to the teacher who had served him like a son for a decade. When they left the house, the teacher howled with pain and struck his head against the wall. It may seem an ominous fall, egged by the spasmodic blasts of destiny, but I know it was more of Uncle's own choice well deliberated as a mathematician.

Uncle stayed all alone in his palatial house during the last four years of his life. A housemaid stayed with her family in the servants quarter. There was a pair of Labradors to fill up whatever was left of the home in the brick and cement structure. During these four years, Uncle would go to Mumbai for a week every month to give lectures at prestigious academies and would return with an attaché case full of money. He was after all much in demand. From Delhi airport he would hire a taxi to reach Dehradoon. And during one of such journeys, Uncle reached home finally, due to cardiac arrest, at the age of sixty two.

ၯၯၯ

Amid continually fevered perceptions and pell-mell severities of modern life, you don't have to cross seven seas to do something purposeful and creative. There is an unperturbed spot of repose within. All of us are endowed with it. Don't get petrified. Don't flinch looking at the tumult. Abandon that haggard and agitated look.

In the brick-paved yard, there are gaps where *peepal* saplings try to get a foothold. A solitary shoot is well trodden over. There is an effort of 'life' to raise its head and expand from every nook corner. The mauled little sapling is a wonder of nature, a fertilized seed in a bird-drop getting a space. It needs your help to retain its wilderness and freedom. If you don't care, it will be trampled to dust again. It needs your support to become a majestic tree some day.

I keep an eye for such orphan saplings and pick them up, half-squashed and plant them in nursery bags. They heal and recuperate with twinkling agility. Why be weary and inarticulate if you cannot break bigger mountains to be a newsmaker? Dig your toes in small openings. Beaming and broad will be your joy. Salvage a little shoot of plant life from getting crushed on a busy pathway or a yard or roadside, plant it in a nursery bag, give it a little dose of love when it's a child and see it maturing into a handsome tree. Then serve yourself papaya slices, toast and piping hot tea tucked away in a corner at a café to celebrate your victory. Ensconced in your celebration, all sweet-faced, rub your hands in anticipation when your tree would have shade for the humans and nesting place and fruits for birds.

ၯၯၯ

These are the times of big things and big issues. If you ride a little vehicle like scooty then you have to accept your humble position and agree to whatever inches of the road by the edges that may be granted to you by the bigger, faster vehicles. A car parked by the side will suddenly take a turn and deprive you of even the thin line of your travel along the road's margin. A window may suddenly pop open giving you the scare of life.

I am going to the town and a liquor lover is asking for a lift. He is standing right in the middle of the road. When he found that I am crossing him without paying heed to his orders, he takes a swipe at my helmeted head. I duck and give myself credit for being alert enough to avoid going dusting at his feet. Further on, you have a non-confident dog looking to cross the road. It almost did what the drunkard had failed to do. Well, there are confident dogs as well, who just step back wisely as you press the horn. By the way, the very same are the categories of the humans crossing the road.

A woman is getting down from the bus with her face backwards and the helpless conductor shouting, 'Look *saamne, saamne!*' She tumbles down as the bus is still in a snaily motion. Luckily, there is no harm done and she gives a sheepish, embarrassed grin. A few people gather around and give her a nice lecture about how to properly get down from a slowly moving bus.

The most challenging task is to avoid a little school boy from scoring a goal. Bored with school after two years of Covid-forced holidays, and not in the habit of attending classes anymore and hence in a terrible mood, he tries to beat his boredom by kicking a coconut shell. He is all for playing football with an empty coconut. My vehicle is surely the goal. I turn sharply at the last moment and he misses it. Misses a goal and kicks dust with a dejected face.

Then I have to overtake a tractor discotheque. The tractor itself makes so much of noise and coupled with huge woofers and speakers it unleashes a tornado. The main beneficiaries of the music, if at all, are those at least a mile off. I cross it with much trepidation. It's almost like getting across a fighter jet.

Randhir, the farmer, is coming back from the town. He feels best while plying his tractor, so in good mood he waves at me. His BP has been recorded to fluctuate between 40 and 240 and he passes off almost every fortnight. But he feels safe while driving his tractor. 'The bumps and jerks keep the body shaking and I am at my best!' he explains the reason for loving tractor riding. So he doesn't miss an opportunity to go plying his tractor.

In the town, the *banjaras* have pitched tents along the road. They have a nice way out to handle the civic body officials. They too want to settle down now after those centuries of wanderings. They have national flags flying from their huts and tents. A few have cows also tethered in front. It stops the civic authorities from treating them merely as stateless ruffians. Nationalism sells well these days and they have as much a right to affirm their credentials as any other internet patriot.

A policeman has parked his car on the road and there is a traffic jam. Many people mutter their grumbling dissent under their breath only. You have to respect police even if they park their private vehicles right in the middle of the road. Small vehicles carry advantages also and I somehow squeeze through.

In the grain market, a merchant shares his philosophy. His servant is busy in cleaning his master's brand new car. The business is slack and there is no work for the servant so the *Lala* has got him to the task of cleaning his already shining car. 'Never leave a servant free!' he tells me the mantra of his success. I get a few moments for a talk with the car-cleaning servant. '*Haan ji ki naukri, Na ji ka ghar!*' he shares his philosophy. Well, both credos seem complementary to each other in the world of business.

If you are lazy to go visiting your town regularly and instead club your multiple tasks in a single visit, you will return at twilight only. There are shrieks and screeching of the noisy spotted owlets as I open the gate. They love jumping out while it's still some minutes left for the fading light of the day and scare the people with their hideous shrieks and squeaks. It sounds like they are condemning my returning in one piece on a little vehicle, riding on a road that has been hijacked by the bigger ones.

Never commit the mistake of being absent for the entire day, especially if there are monkeys around. The garden is vandalized. The banana frond is decimated. It seems an intentional ravage. They are showing the best population growth rate at the moment. There are monkeys-monkeys everywhere. Does nature have a counter? Younger lithe males are trying to break into the established harems of the old rascals. Short on love, a young rascal settled for a very old, shrunk, tailless monkey lady. He was earlier thoroughly bashed up by the huge alpha male so the beaten Romeo settled for a harem discard. If they are off the scene even for an hour, you come to understand what peace really means.

A bat hovers around. The twilight is preponed slightly as it's overcast. It loves to suck juice from the big dark scarlet cone of the banana flower. It seems to love doing *shirashana* as it hangs upside down from the pointed end of the cone. It's miraculous that the cone is still dangling intact after the monkey's free play in the garden.

The kittens are waiting for their milk. They are both males by the way. They now have a cheeky girlfriend. She is very clever. They love her company and their priorities seem to have shifted quite a bit. They have given her an unrestricted access to their milk bowl. They no longer sleep together curled up in a brotherly ball. There is a girl in the equation now. Maybe they are jealous of each other and are looking for some private space.

2

This goes back to the last decade of the last century. Those were the times of very limited means of transport. The last bus would start at half past nine in the night from the district centre for the neighboring district city. Our village fell at a distance of 10 km from the starting point. If the rumble-tumble of circumstances found you stranded at the town at night, you had to muster up every ounce of your flint-hard willpower to get a foothold on the last means of conveyance. If you missed it, pleading a lift with the truck drivers was the last resort. This was lethally inept choice because even if some trucker gave you a lift with a conspicuous condescension, you would lay at the most open disposal of fate as they would be drunk and ply their jangling vehicles with untamed energy.

It was against this background that the last bus acquired a big status. Those were easier times and at half past nine, the town would look deserted like it was midnight. The exotica, the erotica would arrive shaking its tin body with the epitome of teasing virility. It carried an air of romantic freshness as it arrived at long last. The big group of stranded passengers—at that time one would feel like stranded—would welcome it with whistles and catcalls. There would be a stampede to grab the seats. Tempers would ride tautened strings.

There would be dozens of indifferent village drunks among the passengers. Lawlessness went on increasing down the aisle. It reached its peak on the last seat. The conductor looked helpless in doing his ticketing duties. He appeared singlehandedly pitched against millions. He would squeeze through the pandemonium of brawls, lewd songs, guffaws of laughter, cuss words and dirtiest jokes. Free spirit unleashed its lecherous mechanism in full veracity with the evil. Everyone felt so free and independent to go to any extent without the censorial holds of society and traffic laws. Most of the passengers would flatly say 'no' to the bus conductor's request for a ticket. There was no danger of getting caught by the ticket-checking flying squad at night.

There would be a joyful tension and exciting tumult among the law-breaking passengers, and the conductor carried his moist and embittered soul among the enemies. The roadways department chose muscular and brawny types of conductors for this last, tough trip of the day. Amidst the brash and benumbing noise, he tried to salvage some coins in his green leather bag and save the ignominy of not being able to hand out even a single ticket among the crowd. The moment he heard a sorrowful, somber and low-timbred voice, he would swoop down upon the opportunity to sell at least a ticket. More duty-bound types would enter into a verbal spat and even a fistfight with the vagrants. So, all in all, it was a charity round by the roadways. Dozens of passengers on the roof were the freest souls. They were above any rule of society and traffic department. Dark vaults of the sky were the farthest limits for their fun-ride.

Fauji Thekedar, a smalltime construction works contractor, once found him in this pandemonium. He was no *Fauji*, soldier, but his conduct was so orderly and disciplined that they accepted him as a soldier, more real than the real soldiers in the Indian army, and gave him the honorary title of *Fauji*. He also justified this title much demonstratively and crossed the paths and bypaths of personal and professional life with an impressive moral grandstanding.

He felt a mortal strain to his sense of uprightness. Sitting on the last seat amidst the vilest revelers, he decided to teach them a lesson. As the bus stopped at a non-descript station in the countryside, he raised a terrible alarm 'Bomb-Bomb' and made way for the exit as if flying away from definite doom. He fell on the steps with his face down and his back offered a nice ramp for the fellow passengers to escape into the dark outside. The bus was empty within a minute and *Fauji* was the sole passenger lying painfully facedown on the steps. From a distance, they waited eagerly for *Fauji* to be blown away with the bus. There was no blast for five minutes and they slowly came nearer. They got him up and enquired about the bomb. A lot many of them looked eager to start the second installment of punishment. But then a sane voice intervened. 'His back has enough horses galloping on it for the day. Leave him!' He was given a safe corner. Later on, *Fauji* seemed to lose his sense of discipline. He turned cranky and at loggerheads with any sense of order.

ᛒᛒᛒ

This one again dates back to the eighties of the last century. They gave him the name deplume of Bhunda Nai. *Bhunda* derived from his features, which stood as pompous adversaries to any sense of symmetry. There was a gross inaccuracy in their alignment with a sense of normalcy. They shouldn't have named him *Bhunda*, ugly. To me he looked pretty interesting with his strange features. *Nai* was derived from his caste, barber.

Bhunde Nai ka bharota, Bhunda Nai's fodder bundle, was part of local fables. He had spun a dynamic legend about it. Apart from his customary job of cutting hair, shaving beards and filling *hookahs* during weddings, he worked as an agricultural laborer. During those times, in the harvesting season, a laborer would be paid in fixed *maunds* of wheat and fixed number of fodder bales. He couldn't do anything about the wheat because it would be measured. But the equation was open in terms of the number of fodder bales. A bundle could be as big as per the carrying capacity of the bearer. He made it the largest in the area.

He was a small man but very strong in bones. He had sewn himself a huge piece of sackcloth in order to accommodate maximum amount of fodder chaff in a bundle. The people comfortably agreed that his huge piece of cloth could easily accommodate a quintal and half of wheat chaff. Then he would walk like an ant carrying a huge grain of sugar. He was technically entitled to it. As per the norms, the farmer couldn't say no to his load as long as Bhunda could carry it.

Then one day he fell while carrying his load from the farm to his house. They measured the load. It was dangerously near to two quintals. The village headman, a wise old man, had to intervene. 'We have to fix the amount in measurable terms for fodder also, otherwise he would break his neck some day,' he said. So the rule was changed and fodder chaff also came to be fixed in weight so that Bhunda won't put his life at risk by carrying the heaviest load as per the old rule that allowed specified number of bales irrespective of their weight.

Bhunda was disgruntled. 'You higher caste people make rules as per your advantage. What business is it yours if I break my neck while carrying my load,' he cribbed while shaving the beard of a very old farmer. 'We have all the business in doing so and save your life. Don't we take care of our strong bulls who plough the maximum furrows for us?' the old farmer asked in a gentle tone. Bhunda Nai had to agree to the logic. Strong laborers were as much indispensable as the strong bulls in agriculture during those days.

ᗈᗈᗈ

This is October end. There is a ceremonial frenzy of the season through falling leaves, almost a rain of dew at nights, fleecy mist at dawn, dew-drenched flowers at sunrise, paling sunrays, cool breeze, lots of festivals and much welcomed freshness in social mood. The air carries some floating salubrious emotions. Rashe and his younger brother Karne are sitting under a tree. It's day off from work. Well, their case needs a mention here. They have a smalltime, ambling past, a little history of their household.

Rashe's brother Karne went missing at the age of ten. He was spotted last time at the nearest railway station at Sonipat. Everyone accepted that he boarded a train but whether he went north or south nobody had any clue. Well, his parents had three sons and a daughter, so he wasn't missed much in the one-room house of a poor landless family lying almost at the base of the socio-economic hierarchy. The most popular version about him was that his organs had been harnessed by the medical mafia and he had completed his purpose on earth.

His father had one leg afflicted with polio. So they christened him Langda, the lame one. Langda was very hardworking and would give a tough challenge to any two-legged human around in completing tough labor tasks. He loved drinking after the day's hard work. And once he was fully sloshed, he would give a test to his lungs by shouting so loudly as to be heard even in a neighboring village on clear, silent nights. He didn't say too offensive things. He just targeted an ex village head who had denied his request for a below poverty line card that would have made him eligible for free ration and some help for repairing his one-room house. Langda wasn't in the *sarpanch's* good books, so his name didn't enter the beneficiaries, while people far richer than him got their cards that entitled them to receive government subsidies. So Langda would shout 'Dalbir *sarpanch mar gaya!*' throughout the night. It meant the *sarpanch* is dead. The ex village head stayed at the farthest end of the village but he would regularly hear the declaration of his death because Langda shouted better than a big loudspeaker. Finally, they had to give him a few slaps. Langda simply brought down the volume a bit but continued with his declaration nonetheless.

One night a fully drunk Langda was hit by a high-speed car while crossing the road outside the village. The family received ten lakh rupees in compensation from the party in their out of court settlement. That helped them in making a better house. His widow would acknowledge God's help as she saw their better home. 'Thank God their father's bones sold well!' she would say.

Then Karne returned after ten years. He had grown tall like a giraffe. He had actually boarded a train heading north to reach Punjab. There a good-natured Sikh farmer kept him as a helper on his farm. As a goodwill gesture, I gifted them a big speaker lying sullenly in the store. Karne and his brother, Rashe, the gentle giant, loved music. They must have really liked the gift because they played songs at a riotous volume throughout nights. The soul of their father must have felt propitiated, hearing his legacy being carried forward in a nice manner. Rashe and Karne would work on the farms and construction sites and would enjoy ganja whenever possible.

Well, ganja has been quite a popular choice in this part to forget the hardships of life. During the good old days, people would smoke ganja sitting on the last seat of the last bus and its fumes would take everyone in the grip along the aisle. The driver would baulk that his head is spinning and he would crash-land the bus into the roadside ditch. 'Please do it, you will also die with us!' they would encourage him to keep his words.

During those grand old days of theatres, when people danced in front of the screen on popular songs, there would be some ganja-lovers inside the cinema hall who would leave a big plume of ganja smoke leaving dozens coughing and sneezing. Ask them to stop it and they would threaten to help the troubled person by beating him to pass out and hence turn impassive to the offensive smoke. Those were the days when women won't dare to step into a theatre because the crudest words were hurled in the darkness infested with grossly atrophied masculinity. Well, coming back along the ganja strains to the little tale of Rashe's house.

Their brother, named Munna, is a bit higher placed on the scale of cleverness and sophistication in thinking. He works at a needle factory in the nearby town. A few years back he took an overdose of ganja. People said it entered his brain and he shouted all through the nights for almost two years and kept the family tradition of night shouts alive. Well, on a dull drab overcast autumn morning, the song of the birds holds the hope of a bright sun sometime. The fate of the only witty son in the family also got its sunshine. He got his mind back and stopped shouting. In fact, he seems a silent sage now and speaks only the least words required to sustain his job.

Rashe is my favorite of the three. 'How are you Rashe?' I ask. 'Even happier after meeting you,' he replies. He did some work for me and after paying him I asked, 'Is it enough?' 'There cannot be any shortage in your reign,' he replied. He prefers payment in liquor. Handing over the favorite beverage after the completion of another task, I ask him, 'Hope this is sufficient.' He points his fingers to the sky and declares, 'God will definitely give more.' So I have to give him more to fulfill God's wish. He has a cutely slurred speech thanks to the immobility of his lower jaw that went out of action after their horse hit him on jaw when he was an infant.

Their mother is a much-at-ease woman. She is a big lady and moves slowly with ease and comfort. Any type of restlessness is farthest from her persona. She is incapable of holding any ill will against anyone or anything. The villagers take these uncompetitive traits as signs of her foolishness and say that she is weak in mind. Being competitive, restless and quarrelsome are taken as signs of mental health. She is thus beyond any malice. There is an exception though. She has a mission against the monkeys and that makes my head almost bow in reverence before her. The roots of this animosity go back to her childhood. She cannot forget that a monkey snatched away the sweetest mango she has ever tasted in life. Unpardonable. The simians got the duel further when an irritated monkey sank its teeth in her calf muscles. She took hold of its fur and bit even harder. The monkey carried the bite mark to its grave just like she carries hers on her leg.

ᗊᗊᗊ

Through the cut and thrusts of life, as a formal authenticity of my faith, I sometimes go for *Govardhan Parikrama*. Walking miles on naked feet saves the disillusionment from turning into cynicism. Pilgrimages are significant in their psycho-spiritual dimensions. Bleeding hearts and their taut indictment of the covert and overt shades of fate get a respite. The creeping monotony of life withdraws its steps for some time. The sense of peace felt, despite the hardest of moments, is inherently intriguing.

There is a *sadhu* in a wheeled tin cabin stationed along the pilgrimage path. He is reading from a scripture. He looks like a well-kept exotic bird. He has shifty eyes and looks at your hand as you approach him. If your hand doesn't enter your pocket to take the wallet then you are a transgressor into his hymn-citation space. A person not only commits the mistake of not touching his wallet but also performs a double whammy as he tries to click the *sadhu's* picture as if he is clicking a rare bird in a big cage. The *sadhu* loses temper, breaks the sequence of his mantra and retorts, 'I don't take a selfie!'

Nearby a mammoth alpha male is having the fun of his life. He is lying sprawled on the sand, his belly up and all fours spread out. His queens are giving him a nice massage by rummaging their nimble fingers through his fur to pick lice. Another one is busy fulfilling the basic instincts on his queen consort, the primal religiosity of all living beings.

At a path-side temple, the priest proudly informs me that around five crore pilgrims daily visit the temple. The mathematics leaves my head spinning. I try my level best to show that I believe him. I succeed and he pats a nice blessing on my back. It props out something from my wallet. But he doesn't seem too happy about the effect of his blessing pat.

An exclusive signboard says: *Chunmun Bandariya ke liye 1000 jamun ke ped*, meaning one thousand *jamun* trees for Chunmun baby monkey. It's a nice little grove of fruit trees. Blessed be the *Babaji* who asked his disciples to set up this little grove of fruit trees. In fact, many monkeys show that it's fulfilling its intended purpose as they romp around among the fruit trees.

As I get tired while walking, I try to take inspiration from those who cover the entire distance by prostrating, stretching their bodies on the ground all along the way and cover the whole length by measuring it with their bodies. Such flawless faith makes you a God or Goddess without doubt.

᛭᛭᛭

There is a pre-Diwali clean-up in the house. Thanks to the festival spirit, morose strains of discontent and apathy get dispelled from the soul. Loud-mouthed disorder and clumsy disarray get confronted finally. Festivals bestow you a moonlighted spirit and carry a genial touch of humanity. My cleaning the house, as a Lord Ram worshipping Hindu, to welcome Diwali, leaves enough amusing nuggets for the Muslim trash-picker to make him really happy. He is not-a-boy, not-yet-a-man.

Due to the shake-up drive, the crickets are startled, a conference of frogs gets disturbed under a rusty piece of iron, a lazy lizard scurries away as a plastic case is taken out, and spiders struggle on their arthritic, shaky legs as corners are cleaned. The shoebox tied to a not-in-use ceiling fan, fixed to serve as a nest for the birds that never accepted the tenancy offer, has stinging hornets. Well, not all tenants are submissive. They save their house in the cleaning drive. A fighting attitude helps these days.

These are balmy late October days, the autumn holding the little world in cute enticement. The clear sky hanging with a swanky magnanimity. The stars leave a fluorescent nightglow. Peace and harmony hit a peak when the monkeys aren't around. But then some liquor-lover comfortably fills up the vacuum. The wives of the liquor-lovers have to daily stretch their patience to accommodate newer domestic troubles.

There are myriads of anecdotal stories in nature's kitty. A hailstorm strikes to send down the message that not everything is under our control, at least for the time being. It's a heavy lashing by the skies. There are broken branches and decimated paddy in the fields. Who can help it? There are still confusing contours of myriads of mysteries above.

An old alpha male monkey, fuelled by his vintage sexuality, has a child bride towing him these days. How I wish that he gets at least a dozen strikes with big icy clods from the heavens!

The banana cone is still there. Its layers open with gentle succession. A purple sunbird is busy at it during the day. The bats get its possession at nights. The monkeys have stoically spared it so far. They just pluck away little banana fingers as these unfold above the cone.

The little frog in the kitchen seems distraught that the ever-eating Trummp is gone. It was a good source of food. Little crumbs would fall from the cage and the little frog would dine under the cage. The gluttonous parrot proudly looked at the tiny frog below. Well, that reminds me of Trummp again. I missed to mention that as it finally emerged from its charming spell about eating and emerged from the cage, I shouted, '*Ja Shimran jee le apni zindagi!*' Let's hope she is having a nice nuptial inning with her husband. I would prefer to call it Shimran now because there is no need of using cuss words now.

It reminds me of another parrot. My brother's friend has a pet parrot in Kashmir. It drinks wine with his retired father in the evenings and after that in eased-up spirits whistles at any woman who comes visiting the house. He isn't bothered about the men entering the house. Maybe the cosmic sense of masculinity itself carries the strains of lecherousness.

Mistri Sat Prakash, a native of Jhansi, informs that the parrots born on an old, grandfatherly *neem* tree are wise and clever and can be taught to speak. But those born on *mahua* trees are dimwits and enjoy their foolish *tete-tete* only.

Sat Prakash is helping me restore a semblance of order in the dilapidated and disarrayed yard. The bricklayer is a small frail man with strong hands. The latter fact is more important for a mason because only strong hands enable you to keep grasping at life, especially if you are poor and have to work daily to survive.

Last night, after he had finished his work for the day in my yard, a smart teacher lured him and others to transfer his provisions to the town. 'It will take just an hour,' he told them. But that one hour got completed at three in the morning. So he and his helper are sleepy as they work for me on the next day. They work very lazily and I allow them their semi-sleep. Exploitation there has to be compensated here with some lenience now. It helps people in keeping their faith in humanity.

He is extremely soft spoken and a simple man. You point out the most glaring fault in what he has done, he will listen to you very patiently; he would continue listening though your suggested solution and would finally add, very gently, that this is exactly what he was going to do. His best quality is that he doesn't trouble his brains with his own plans as a mason. He would do exactly what you tell him to do.

In his sleepy state, taking the afternoon tea, to make up for the inefficiency at work during the day, he gives me new nuggets of information. 'A *prêt* has just three of the five primal elements, a sort of spooky concoction of air, sky and ether. So we shouldn't worry too much about them. They lack solidity and ground to do something physical directly,' he informs me. Well, that makes the ghosts pretty harmless to me now. It seems a highly scientific explanation.

His helper is big built, very suitable for the physical tasks of digging, lifting load, mixing concrete and the rest of ilk that a mason expertly orders his helper to do. The boy is smeared with soil and cement and grumbles about his slovenliness. 'Who has ever washed a lion's face?; who has washed a male buffalo's behind?' Sat Prakash eggs him on, making him a lion and a robust buffalo both at the same time.

Despite all the strength of his hands, his handshake carries a feather touch. It feels like you are holding a lifeless hand. It seems he has shaken hands for the first time in the late fifties of his life. Who shakes hands with them? The people usually shake and jolt the littlest semblance of dignity and respect their soul still carry.

And irrespective of the day's concretely frank and upfront tidings, the nights can be gentle, affable if you have the aesthetic signpost of some slow-paced, gently characterized Iranian movie to guide your way through the night's oeuvre. The Iranian movie 'A Cold Day' is another warm, little story. To like an Iranian movie, you need to be a lover of small-time beauty of nature, hills, flowers, streams; the unhurried pace of life; smiles, soft emotions, simplicity of life and dollops of nature. They beautifully make up for the absence of song and drama.

It's a little school among small, rolling hills. A teacher saves a little second grader from the fire in the school and gets serious burn injuries. Little Ali is the boy concerned. He is plagued with self-reproach as the teachers blame him for the episode. The teacher has burns on his face and is hesitant to appear before the students. Ali breaks the ice by visiting the teacher who has gone into utter isolation on account of his changed looks. They face each other with frankness, dignity and respect. The smiles return.

ᐅᐅᐅ

Like a submissive protagonist in the seasonal play directed by nature, late autumn is handing over the baton to early winter. A rufous treepie, a dweller of the hills and now here for the winter stay, is seen on the *gulmohar* tree, picking dry ends of the branches to make a nest. Their distinct sound sails over the chirpy songs of the resident species with a palpable dissonance. The migratory couple is exploring a suitable nesting site among a clump of trees in the courtyard of an unoccupied house in the neighborhood. They but see a lot of monkeys in the locality and sensing the dangers born of the simian mischief they abandon the plan. Common sense seems their handmaiden. Ours seems a pale imitation of the unadulterated sense found among the non-human species.

Rockchats are very unassuming and non-pompous birds. A rockchat couple prefers to fly into the verandah to pick ants, spiders and even baby lizards if they are lucky on their menu for the day. They sometimes hop into the room and with an anecdotal perch stare into the dressing table glass with a mysterious clarity and certitude. The couple seems very happy in spending their days hopping and flying in the garden, yard and verandahs. It's a silent, non-interfering bird. It's nice to have them around. Both of them somehow add to the silence and solitude around me.

Even early winter has soaring daytime temperature. You can feel the heat. But the putative votaries of superstardom, the lethal shenanigans, the perpetrators of ideological excesses are busy in building hypersonic missiles. China is desperately scavenging for superpower status. They are taking *panga* with everyone around. It looks a myopic venture. I think they have preponed their jump onto the hot seat by a decade. They could have waited for some more time. Amidst all these bleeding-heart clichés, climate change is too common an issue to grab anyone's attention. So the planet keeps smoldering.

But still as an ode to the autumn, dry *neem* leaves drizzle down carrying the nostalgic nuances of better times when autumns were real autumns, not just in name like now. What is a dry *neem* leaf by the way? It's but a bit naughty dust that rustles and rollers over; a kind of bit of earth flying for some fun. While, a flying bird is almost a visible representative of air.

In the *curry patta* leaves, there is a tiny ball of honeybees and near it a nest of spotted doves. It's a peaceful and patient couple. They seem to have waited on the sidelines as other bird couples stole the procreative show during the monsoons. They reserved their love for late autumn and now slowly walk onto the stage.

The banana flower cone has oriental white eyes also. It's a beautiful, tiny, light-green bird with a white ring around their eyes. Beyond the bloodthirsty beats of the human civilization, they are happy taking little sips from the dangling scarlet banana cone. In the mornings, there are beads of dew on the cone and these little birds just love breakfasting upon them.

ॐॐॐ

Rashe fell like a log after drinking too much. He carries a bloody, self-healing scar on his temple. I point it out and he informs me, 'I have promised myself not to drink anymore.' 'When did you make the promise?' I ask. 'Yesterday,' he answers. 'Should I distribute *prasad* that Rashe has quit drinking?' I ask him. 'Please wait! Even if I quit, others won't allow me to stand by my decision,' he says and looks at his friend standing nearby. The promise met its end on the second day and he celebrated the evening in the usual way. 'But I promise not to fall anymore,' he said to me the next day.

Rashe is strictly against hoarding anything and would take only as much as it fulfills his requirements at the moment. A meditative present-moment liveliness. Offer him something extra and he says, 'But there is no need of it.' Ganja and liquor are an exception though. He would take as much as you offer. I tried to force an extra kitchen stand and a redundant, but in perfect condition, ceiling-high tin tank for wheat storage. Someone in his place would have smartly calculated their resale values and would have happily grabbed the opportunity even if these weren't needed in his house. But Rashe is beyond such calculations. He rejects the offer because he doesn't need them. And schemes like taking them and selling aren't appealing to him. He but carefully inspects two aluminum pots, suspiciously scans them and says his mother will welcome them in her kitchen. The kitchen stand is squarely rejected.

I leave it in front of my gate and when I go to check it after fifteen minutes, it's missing. Someone in need, or even sheer greed, has taken it.

᠈᠈᠈

Dhillu is an agonizingly disciplined man. His life's show falls under the rubric of 'what will people say?' He holds the pole of reputation as he walks on the rope of life. His core ideological moorings keep him safe in the bay beyond controversies and bad name. He is but flabbergasted about the uncaring ways of the current generation. 'Imagine what the world has come to be. Yesterday I overheard a few boys talking. "You don't speak! You got slapped for your conduct. It was such a big insult and humiliation. You must be ashamed of it," said one of them. But the champion replies, "What is insult? This so-called shame, insult or humiliation lasts just two minutes. After that it has no business to be in one's mind." Imagine what hard skins for such tender age. With this type of attitude, will anything stop them from crossing any limits?' He is scandalized and seems very much disturbed. Maybe he realizes that he has led his life in a completely unfit way.

᠈᠈᠈

The other day, *Balbir ki bahu*, a poor woman on the socio-economic hierarchy, died. In patriarchy, you are mostly known as someone's wife. Very few people know a woman's real name. She was suffering and prematurely aged beyond her years. But then something rich happened during her last journey. As her *arthi* passed on the road on the way to the cremation ground, a sweets-laden tempo of a sweet-maker goofed it up. Trays of freshly prepared *laddoos* went falling in a line along the way. She went floating over the *laddoos. Laddoos* in place of flowers isn't a bad bargain. Many dogs felt grateful as they feasted upon the chancy offering.

Before setting her onto the last lag in the journey, i.e., setting fire to the pyre, it was observed that her gold nose-stud was still in her occupation. Her son tried to salvage the last worldly possession but it won't come off. He pulled very hard but the skin on the old woman's proud nose stood ground. He had to leave it. Maybe she loved her nose-stud and carried it with her to the other world.

ॐॐॐ

Early November is the best part of the year for me. This part of the year is seminally fresh. You can see through the transparent liveliness. The river of time is slowly meandering carrying little buoyant waves. The early winter is so relaxed, playful and carefree in its pre-puberty days.

The roses sway in gentle cool breeze. In salubrious early November, the flowers blossom up fully, open up their self completely, then willingly scatter their petals without pain and suffering. They kiss the ground with as much passion as they blew kisses for the air. Look at them carefully, they greet you and acknowledge your presence with a fragrant smile.

Little pinwheel-shaped *Parijat* flowers carpet the yard in the morning. The small-sized tree has a distinctive place in Hindu mythology. The holy tree lets loose a fine drizzle of highly fragrant little white flowers as the sun peeks over a dewy, misty morning.

The dew-kissed marigolds are sturdy. They stay for a few days. In garlanded form, they make sporadic forays into mythology.

A skink crawls slipperily on the floor, sneaks under a flowerpot and bumps into a lizard. Both of them then run for their lives in opposite directions.

The loveliest roses are nourished by dewy nights, balmy sunrays and gentle breeze. I have enough flowers to sustain the little ball of honeybees. They have lost their orchards and gone are big honeycombs, so even a small ball of honeycomb is welcome. It's better than none at all. The little ball of honeybees must be feeling in a paradise with showers of night-blooming jasmine flowers so nearby. They get busy on a very early breakfast. They are whizzing about amid booze and gossip.

The ground gets carpeted with white flowers under the *Parijat*. I usually collect them and put them in the flowerbed so that they don't get trampled. I find it a sin to trample a flower. The flowers then become celebratory lunch for scores of little insects.

The spotted doves and the honeybees are very cordial neighbors. The lazy cat now sleeps under the tree. Most probably, he has seen the nest. I hope the bees will teach him a lesson if he troubles their docile neighbor. Sadly, the doves are very lazy in the nest-making art. It's a poor, fragile, unkempt, clumsy nest. It's situated at a perfectly reachable height, making it a treat for any winged or even earthly predator. Looking at their careless, almost foolish ways, I sometimes wonder how do they even survive as a species.

The banana flower cone welcomes all from the sweetest ones like butterflies to the stingiest ones like yellow hornets. Nature doesn't mind it much because they take only as much as they need. The scarlet cone having nutritious sap is placed on the open platter for all to take their share.

There are earthworms in the garden. They are very near to earth, hence named as such. They are just a bit more conscious earth. The earth that crawls a bit. They crawl, die, decay and become perfect earth very soon.

These are beautiful days. The dusk descends suddenly. A little group of scaled munias is raising a feeble ruckus—they cannot turn noisy even in their worst mood. A hawk is after one of them. Maybe it's a young hatchling that is yet to learn the entire set of flying maneuvers or perhaps it's an old one with tired wings. It dives into a clump of trees, followed by the hawk. I can hear a painful screeching sound. Most probably, it's a successful hunt or a failed escape.

Camouflaged by the shades of the falling dusk, the lazy cat crawls up the tree very cautiously. The silverbills, tailorbirds and oriental white eyes raise a protest. The dove keeps sitting in its poor nest, believing itself to be invisible. It but flew away at the last moment as the cat easily crept up to the nest. The hungry cat reached the nest and got a crunchy early dinner. The dove kept mum at night but cried through the next day. But it turned silent by the evening. The tragedy was almost scripted beforehand given their lazy and slovenly attempt at nest making. It was destined that the cat would have a breakfast, lunch or dinner any time. Its early foray means that it had a small meal. Had it waited for some days, the food would have been feistier. But then they don't think like we humans. They live in the present.

Beyond the mainstream pruning and trimming, it may sound a sidelined, marginalized narrative but it carries its wholesome spiritual trail and healthy cultural pulse. Modern life is stacked from floor to ceiling, pushing us into musty corners of our own creation. The money-spinning fancy footwork, the mad scrambling for supercilious slice barely leaves any shelf space for little innocent smirks, casual banter and childish merry-go-rounds.

ﮠﮠﮠ

Diwali falls in the first week of November. The government is trying its level best to curb pollution on the occasion of our grand festival. The firecrackers are banned. But a liquor-lover sets up a huge fire of tyres to meet the shortage of firecrackers. The entire village is wrapped in a thick, black shroud of smoke. All this happens during the day. He has set the nighttime tempo for the firecrackers from the black market.

In the town, sweetmeats are more ubiquitous than grocery items on the festive occasion. Even a puncture shop has sweets piled up on a table in front of it. The *puncturewala*-turned-sweetmaker even said a firm 'no' to my request for an air fill in the tyre of my scooty. 'There is no air in the tank,' he told me with an injured pride for not taking him as a full *mithaiwala*. 'Take *mithai*,' he offers. I have to move on with my half-deflated tyre.

In the town, almost three-fourth of the road's width is occupied by the sweet vendors displaying their items. Almost every outlet has throngs of shoppers.

The snake charmers are forbidden from keeping snakes in their baskets these days. In order to collect charity money, they are clad like yogis and play their gourd flutes, *been*, in front of the stacks of sweets as if a snake would surface from the clods of sugary sweetmeats. By the way, presently sugar seems even more dangerous than snakes to the humans. So they have a nice replacement for the snake hoods.

Despite the ban on firecrackers to save Delhi from pollution, there are more crackers available in the black market than the normal one. There is an illicit fun in cracking dummy bombs and firing toy guns. Pungent smoke covers the sky. Eyes burn and you can feel the smoke going straight into your lungs. How wonderful it would be if we celebrated Diwali in its real spirit instead of just letter-driven lip service.

I put an oil lamp under the *Parijat* tree. It glowed for fifteen hours. In the morning, it seemed as if the tree has paid it a homage with a drizzle of flowers around it. The post-Diwali morning carried a heavy layer of smog. A cold, shivery, metallic blanket holding the fates of our lungs in its tight grip. Imagine, there are still climate change skeptics. Thankfully, a breeze rolled up and dispelled the post-celebration gloom.

The black-market bombs do one nice thing. As they give a blast, the monkeys think that we have started a war against them. Hence, they are on the back-foot for the time being.

ᢩᢩᢩ

A small group of Sikh farmers still carries the farmer agitation on the Singhu border. A *nihang* Sikh comes visiting the market from the protest site. The blue-robed warrior of Sikhism is seen at an Airtel service centre. His old-looking base mobile set isn't working. He offers it to the elegantly dressed lady on the counter. 'You keep it and give me a new one. This one might be of some use to you,' he says. How I wish this world was as simple as this man of religion thinks it to be.

ᢩᢩᢩ

My Sufism-loving father gave me the nickname of Sufi. But the bucolic tongues twist it to Suppi, Scoopi, Soopi and scores of many other rustic derivates. There are just three or four people in the village who can pronounce my name properly. *Tau* Surje thought I was Sukhi Ram, so called me Sookhi. Then there were a few old *taus* who called me Subbi.

꘠꘠꘠

Tau Hoshiyar Singh is in his nineties now and is almost deaf and nearly blind. '*Tau*, can you recognize me?' I ask him. 'Yes,' he says, trying to sound confident, his mind already working on the problem. 'Then tell, who am I?' I put up the teaser. 'Pappu,' he says. 'See, you cannot see at all,' I try to make him confess that he cannot see. 'Yea, I meant to say Suppi's brother,' he hasn't lost the confidence in the least. Does he mean to say I'm my own brother or he has recognized me as my brother? 'But you said Pappu,' I try to make him flinch from his firm perch. 'Yea, It's the same,' he says coolly.

꘠꘠꘠

Those were diminutive, sleepy times in the eighties of our childhood during the last century. Now after almost four decades, little-little memories peek over gentle facades. I must be eight or nine. I was walking by the pot-holed district road on the way to our fields about a kilometer and half from the village. The little tales in schoolbooks with their moral lessons, at least during those times, laid a complex and experiential field to test the lessons.

I was also put into a predicament. I found a fifty-paisa coin. My brisk pacing got slowed down. I had to avoid moral bankruptcy. A fifty-paisa coin carried enough weight till that time. It would fetch ten sugar candies or even fifty little buttons of candies that came one for a paisa. I carried it in my firm, warm, moist, tight fist. Candies would make the day of any child any day in any age. I hope they still carry the same charm.

Still it wasn't my money. I knew by rote learning that one should be honest and should try to return the lost money to the owner. I saw a group of girls cutting wood by the road and instantly the opportunity to clear my conscience arose. 'Has anyone of you lost a fifty-paisa coin?' I asked them. I was expecting a no but one of them said yes. It dumped my spirits. The coin seemed to be glued to my palm. 'Tell me where did you lose it?' I raised the level of my enquiry. She was a very intelligent girl. 'Anywhere between that point and the village school on the road,' she swiped her little axe along the road to cover two kilometers of stretch. Under the spell of mouth-watering candies, morals can be stretched. I elongated my next query along the lengthened morals. 'Tell me the year on it,' I asked. To clear my conscience she had to fail in the test. She hazarded a guess that came to be wrong. So there I carried my coin with a clear conscience and in full honesty.

3

As per the theory of relativity, time was slower during our growing up years. It left much time at the villagers' disposal to while it away in *chaupal* gossips and idle talks over hookah and cards. Grandfather loved mathematics. Since almonds strengthen the brain, from where the sprouts of mathematics originate, he loved almonds as well. So we siblings would break almond shells in the open yard in front of our house. In a bucolic world thirsty for happenings, it presented an interesting episode. The neighbors would creep out and sit around. They counted the number of almond shells broken. Then all of them had interesting bits of information to share about the best way to hit to break the shell cleanly. Just imagine the amount of time at our disposal during those years.

Beyond emotional unleashment on the issue, alcohol mints a lot of revenue for the government. With its firm moorings in history, the liquor industry is progressing really well. Now we have as many liquor-lovers roaming around during the day as we had earlier during the nights. The booze business is going great guns as more and more people lose their spirits. One of the liquor-lovers is determined to turn everyone deaf by playing the loudest music for 18 hours non-stop. Then he fell senseless around midnight. The tortured speakers got a well-deserved rest. But our ears carried the echo still drumming in our ears. And when it would come to an end, he would be back with a louder bang.

ᑭᑭᑭ

It's a wish to go slow and continue writing peacefully about small, small things of life till a ripe old age. God, please don't rock and toss my boat with sudden throws and challenges. I'm more like a dove. I don't want to go too fast and too far. I just want to move slowly with a smile. The miles covered don't matter. I just wish to be there like a sagely old tree with crooked, hollow trunk and still waiting for another spring for some more shoots and tender leaves on the hardened, dry branches. A little place of rest and repose for some old birds at least, if not the young ones.

ᑭᑭᑭ

An industrious cat will go for a rat. A lazy one will crawl among the trees to steal dove eggs, the easy catch. As we have seen, the lazy cat had an early dinner of dove eggs the other day. The dove cried the next day and to give herself some happiness laid another egg on the following day. By the way, they lay eggs in a little series, separated by a few days gap.

Everything is relative. The dove is still lazier than the cat, so it's a win-win situation for the idle cat. It again crawled for another early dinner, too early this time. I was in the yard when the tailorbird raised a ruckus like a good neighbor. The honeybees didn't have any issue like the last time. They leave it for the cat and the dove to sort it out among themselves. So they stayed neutral. I don't think the honeybees and the cat compete for anything regarding food, otherwise they will also sting, if not speak out like the tailorbird. The cat doesn't seem to have any appetite for honey. A lesson here. It's advisable to have some common interests with one's neighbors so that at least they speak out when you are in a soup. This repetition of crime got me into good neighborly emotions. The egg dropped with a plop followed by the lustily hungry cat. My stick dispensed justice and away went the cat scared out of its wits. It didn't return the next day but I was sure of its return because it loved its milk bowl, being too lazy to hunt rats. It would maintain some distance for a couple of days and again get into the usual business.

ᐅᐅᐅ

Darkling beetle isn't named after its dark color. It's a gray ground beetle that loves to stay in the dark. Its Latin name means 'seeker of dark places and trickster'. But some are active during the day also. They are generalistic omnivores feeding on rotting wood, decaying leaves, dead insects, fresh plant matter, fungi, larvae and much more that we hardly have any clues about.

It's an unpretentious armored beetle. Under the sunlight, as per the scheme in the beetle world, it would count as travelling by the night. Nights carry risks for us. The same is during the day for these nocturnal insects.

Even while at a run, it seems a leisure walk, something like a jolly, happily portly twaddle of a rotund gentleman. It crossed the garden, walked across the courtyard, walked up to the floored inner yard. As I came nearer, it feigned a perfected death. I moved away and it abandoned its acting and started again.

It looks an adventurous beetle on a long walk. A carpenter ant comes from the opposite direction. They stand face to face, greet each other, shake their antennae to convey bye and move on. An ant—far smaller—hurries past from behind. The ground beetle doesn't care. It loves it gentle, leisurely pace. Another carpenter ant also goes speeding up as it overtakes and takes a U-turn after going a few yards. What is the use of speed if you aren't sure of the direction? It's better to go slowly with a clear sense of direction. The returning ant is in much hurry, so forgets to greet the gentleman like the earlier ant did.

The ground beetle tries a hop but seems a funny miniature version of a rhino on slow trot. It but realizes its mistake and goes back to its natural pace. There it crosses the inner yard and arrives at a hole in a corner. It's a nice, cozy, secure hole in the flooring. It seems an ideal spot for a hiatus. It snoozes around the opening. A skink raises objection at the encroachment. The beetle is too big for her mouth and she herself is out of reach for the beetle. So there is no confrontation.

It tries to climb the wall, goes with the slowest of a cautious crawl like an expert mountaineer sticking to a sheer rock face. It realizes that heights aren't for it and wisely comes down. A very wise decision indeed, a proper estimation of its abilities. It then moves cautiously, slanted over the edge of a stone slab. A journeyman on the move, it goes into the verandah, then into the room. Who am I to stop its march? I can just look at it.

ᐳᐳᐳ

Hope you remember the spotted dove episode? The broken nest is still there. Without any doubt, all doves are very lazy. They seem content in their small, peaceful world and take the trouble to coo sometimes and walk with gentle strides. They show a bit of urgency only when they take off. They flutter their wings pretty loudly to even scare you sometimes. In comparison to their eased living, a tailorbird looks weary and stress-battered.

The nest is just an assemblage of few dry twigs at a height where you can easily touch it with your extended hand and raised heels. A pair of laughing dove now decides to occupy the abandoned house. They aren't deterred by the painful recent past. They make some flimsy, make-believe adjustments to the arrangement of twigs. You can literally see through the nest when you stand under it and scan it for its safety features.

A honey buzzard lands onto the small *curry patta* tree bearing the nest and the honeycomb. The birds haven't laid eggs yet. They fly with a loud beating of wings. The nest is empty but he gets a bonus, the little ball of honeybees. It's a small hive because flowers are vanishing from the planet and my little garden is sufficient for a tiny hive only. But the eagle gets a little sweet beakful of honey. The dove couple looks adamant and returns after some time. They will surely lay eggs despite cats and the eagle stalking them. They are into it with a single-minded focus. In between, some biggest favor by luck favors them with a successful hatching. However, given their lazy ways, it seems a miracle almost.

𐤐𐤐𐤐

A decade back, I once took a photo of one of the *taus* in our village. 'I know why are you taking my photo,' he said as I clicked the picture. 'Why?' I asked. 'Because you think I'm just about to die and you will be able to see my face later,' he looked hurt.

He is still around after ten years and most importantly can see reasonably well. I need to take his latest photo so

I approach him. He is near the century of years and loves cricketers hitting centuries. He loves those who meet the three-figure mark and hates those who get out in the nineties. He hates them even more than who get out on zero.

He was watching an IPL match. That was the time when luscious cheer-girls danced in skimpy skirts to celebrate the hits to the boundary. I am not sure whether he loves the boundaries more or the dance. I think both of them cheer him up. Once after a hit to the fence they forgot to show the dance. He looked very disturbed and the next boundary took a few more overs in coming. He grew impatient and jittery. 'Why would they hit boundaries if the girls turn lazy and don't dance? The girls didn't dance on the last hit,' he held a grouse against the girls.

He had another issue about them showing the same dancing reward for both fours and sixes. 'They should do something better for a sixer, which is far better than a four,' he reasoned. I was about to say, 'Do you want the skirts to go up *tau* to celebrate sixers?' But I kept the query hidden within me because in that case he would have surely taken a sixer-type swipe at my legs with his well-oiled stick.

ᗥᗥᗥ

In the past, an old man's wife found fresh dose of love in her late fifties. She ditched him and eloped with her middle-aged lover, leaving behind a brood of five grown up men and women, two of them already having little children of their own. I happen to overhear a row between the old man, in his eighties now, and his graying son. They are very angry at each other. 'Your wife ran away with someone. You are fit for nothing,' the son probes his fingers in the hurtful corner of the old man's heart. 'And your mother eloped with a goon,' the old man countered. Then both of them turned silent under the weight of the family history.

ᗡᗡᗡ

A guy married very late, at the age of forty in fact. In the conservative village society, it's almost like getting married while you are peeping into your grave. They would love child marriages any day. His classmate in the village school meets him after a few years. 'I hardly meant to marry but this society, peer pressure, and family and relatives nagging my soul day and night forced me into marriage at last. I couldn't handle it anymore. It was like they had put the end of a stick into my bum and held it to maneuver around,' he lamented. 'And now by agreeing to get married, you have allowed the stick to be entirely thrust inside you, so carry it smartly now,' the friend quipped matter of factly.

ᗡᗡᗡ

She is a new bride, pretty looking, slender and curvaceous with a biting pout on her lips. Whatever energy is left after the night revelries driven by the youthful passion, she spends it on her mother-in-law. The old woman has a loafy, gruffy, rumbling tone that booms in a dull way. It's highly inept for fighting. The young woman, on the other hand, is incisive like a knife. Her high-pitched, sharp notes cut through the buttery, loafy resistance of her mother-in-law. Who wins is a foregone conclusion. She easily tames the old woman during the day. For the nights, her pretty face and slender figure is more than sufficient to tame the already exhausted husband who works in a needle factory in a nearby town. He is well aware of the dangers presented by small, sharp, incisive things. And thus starts another little story of lengthening another pedigree.

ᐁᐁᐁ

Many decades back, it was a scrub forest in the countryside surrounding my village. The distances were still measured by creaking cartwheels even though rolling tyres had made their presence felt. A *sanyasi* meditated in a little cave dug into an earthen mound overlooking a little pool of water in the scrub forest. As he meditated, a wolf and a cobra stayed nearby. He achieved enlightenment. Now we have the holy pond surrounded by a tiny grove of banyan, *peepal* and *neem* trees.

The place carries its mystique and solitariness, where one can still feel the aromatic wafts of the holy man's spirituality. There is an elemental sound of faith reverberating through the gusts of breeze playing with the leaves. Silence and peace is unperturbed as the moments pass in tuneful glides with harmony. Birds have a melodious regaling among the trees. A family of green pigeons safely coos in the banyan canopy. There is a group of fourteen geese that own the pond waters and they assert their rights pretty noisily now and then.

The holy man used to bathe in the tiny pond. Faith is feisty, disarming and daring. Our own self is its mighty nurturer. The waters in the little pond heal skin allergies. Many people have been cured and the myth stays with the little mossy pool.

In the little shrine commemorating the holy man, a priest draws healing powers from the holy man's legacy. He acts as a faith healer and his simple process of chanting mantras and blessings—drawing sustenance from the holy man's spiritual energies—cures people of typhoid. Many people authenticate the efficacy of this faith-healing treatment. Long lasting are the effects of meditations.

The place has all that it takes for the seekers of silence and peace. The offerings at the little temple sustain birds and a few dogs on the premises. The seeds of penance leave behind a crop that serves humanity, and some animals and birds also, for a long time.

༄༄༄

There is nostalgia and romance in the air in early November. A festive spirit is daintily festooned to most of the faces. There is love in the air. A butterfly couple flies in looping, free patterns of companionship, love, lust and procreation. It represents the air's gallant, love-drenched, unhurried, effortless, soaring spirits.

The rose petals are velvety, soft, scented and scatter to playful winds after their short dazzle on the stage of existence. They are like a pampered princess. Marigolds, on the other hand, are hardy ones. Their lack of flashy colors and intoxicating smell is compensated by hardiness and durability. They are like hardworking, working class people. No wonder, the Gods prefer them as garlands around their necks.

A *peepal* that I planted has grown too long. Its thin stem looks too eager to kiss the skies. But too soaring ambitions see us plummeting down to kiss the ground as well. The lanky plant falls under the weight of its own tall aspirations. It now needs the support of a stick to regain its vertical. Helping a bent down plant to hold its head high is a nice thing to do. I only advise the plant to go up at a moderate, manageable pace.

༄༄༄

If your being isn't bugged with ambition to a specific extent, the institutions, people, society, even your own family will find you weak and inefficient for their scheme. Satti Bhai, my cousin brother, is a clear example of this. He held a governmental job but had no hunger to rise in the ranks. During his youth, he loved mountaineering but the Himalayas lost their charm as drinking became his primary love in the evenings. He is a thorough gentleman in the art of drinking. Even after the alcohol's chauvinistic liberality running in his veins, he is always at peace with one and all. As the bottle hits the bottom, he is a replica of some inclusionist, flexible, eclectic and absorptive God.

But then something happened that spoilt the equilibrium. I saw him losing his temper for the first time. It wasn't after drinking. It was in broad daylight when his body was free of liquor. We were standing in a narrow, crowded old Delhi bazaar lane. Electric cables above, just a few feet above one's head, crisscrossed the narrow space like thick creepers to give the sense of a false ceiling. Satti Bhai stood with a sense of aloofness and majestic muse about the futility of all this scurrying about, probably already looking up to the evening when his already slow world would become almost stand-still in the beautiful fog created by the bottle.

Then the leisurely strolling moments were checkmated. A monkey was kingly sitting on the electric cables, its legs dangling above Satti Bhai's head. With an unbelievable ease, it peed on his head. As the warm fluid trickled down his crown, Satti Bhai couldn't believe the attack on his sagely dignity. He yelled revengefully, baulked a terrible cuss word and jumped to hold the monkey's tale to swing it and thrash it around. The offending rascal easily escaped leaving Satti Bhai out of words and fuming with rage.

Later, he took bath and shampooed his hair but, as he said, the bad smell won't go. He got a terrible headache

A NOBODY'S NOTEBOOK

as well, which he said was due to the horrible chemicals in the simian pee. That evening, the bottle failed to sober him down for the first time. He was snappy, moody and argumentative. That was his initiation into after-drinking usual kind of revelry. He is capable of punching his co-drinkers these days. So primarily what happens to us can mould us into countless variants.

𐤐𐤐𐤐

We called him Kori but his real name was Vinod. His mother was from our village and he came visiting his maternal granny's house during school vacations.

Those were slow-paced times. We got our lessons in animal care and kindness through simple norms and traditions. When stray female dogs in the streets gave birth to puppies, we would prepare nice little kennels for them using paddy haylofts. As the canine lady in labor rested, in the evenings we set out on a sort of alms-asking sortie on behalf of her. The group of children would hold an earthen pot, bowl or basin, little fingers holding the rim from all sides and there we went yelling in front of closed doors, raising a ruckus. People would offer chapattis, *subzi*, curd, buttermilk, millet *khichdi* and other rustic attempts at cooking a supper. All of it would be dumped in the same container to make it a heady cocktail of a canine supper. It would acquire a unique flavor as layers of different items entered the recipe.

Kori was involved in one such sortie. He loved *bajra khichdi* and buttermilk to along with it. It was a winter night. Those were the days when the streets were dark after the sunset and electricity arrived just in name, so most of the houses had candles and kerosene lamps. Kori must have felt very hungry. On top of that, his favorite dish was in the pot. He was draped in a shawl and in the dark helped himself with plenty of handfuls of buttermilk laced *bajra khichdi*. In fact, he chucked it out clean. So this part of the collective food went missing.

Standing in front of a door from where the incharge boy tilted the basin to check whether the collection was sufficient. To his puzzlement, the *khichdi* part of the canine supper was missing. It was pretty spooky and left us wondering about some ghost taking it away. We had a scary discussion about ghosts stealing *bajra khichdi*. Kori played a lead role in spreading the spooky tales about certain *djins* and *prets* who loved this food as his grandfather had told him.

A few days later, having nicely digested the *khichdi*, but unable to digest the secret, Kori told me, on promise of keeping it a secret of course, that he had availed himself with that part because he liked it and we were late for dinner that day. Commendably, he had managed it very smartly, even though it was dark, from a basin that was held by many fingers.

Once, during some other summertime school break, he arrived at his granny's place. Driven by his curiosity about his anatomy, he had an injured hung. So he couldn't use his pants. He wore a *lungi*. Moreover, his rubber slippers went sailing down the village canal during one of the fun-bathing episodes, leaving him the option of wearing his maternal uncle's leather boots that were double his size. In a *lungi* and double-sized black boots, he looked the kingpin of local goons. This, and his injured hung, gave him the walk of a teasing swag, a kind of flirtatious swaying gait. An old woman next door took it to her heart. He turned an eyesore to her and she cracked jibes at him. 'He hardly has any legs in his bum but look at his attitude,' she would say loudly whenever Kori passed her house.

With an injured pride, and injured hung, Kori resolved to take a revenge. He started relieving himself—in both solid and fluvial sense—on their own roof. When his granny found the roof turned into an open toilet, Kori pointed out the enemy old woman, saying he had seen her scaling the low parapet dividing their roofs and performing the relieving rites. But his granny cackled with laughter. Much concerned, Kori asked, 'Why, you don't believe me? Then whom do you suspect?' 'I don't just suspect but I have full knowledge that it's you. It's a boy's poop of your age *beta*,' she spoke wisely. So the attempt at taking revenge failed.

ᕿᕿᕿ

Maybe after flying for many a fruitless mile, the honey buzzer has spotted the little honeycomb in our garden. In a world of vanishing flowers and rapidly decreasing honeycombs, it has a right to take a little bite of the thing that gives it a name. The attempt turns out to be very clumsy. The majestic honey-loving hawk is too big for the delicate branches of the small curry-leaf tree. The hunter has to grab its morsel while almost in flight. A bigger piece falls on the ground than what it takes away. But they don't get sullen over such drops and misses. They are happy to take whatever falls in their kitty. The notion of getting more or something going waste doesn't turn their head heavy. The honeybees struggle over the fallen piece. Instead of complaining over the loss, they use their energy to retrieve the grounded granules of honey. After a labor of one hour, they settle for almost the same shape as before. It's so easy to move on with life if one doesn't carry the extra load of grudges, guilt and anger.

The purple cone of banana flower hangs with silent, pinpointing precision. It's heavy enough to tilt the stem and hangs down like a mason's iron-cone used to check the vertical component of the wall under construction. It's ideally, from our economical point of view, supposed to be taken off once the gap between the last row of the banana fingers and the flower cone is 15 cm because it sucks a lot of nutrition from the tree. But I keep it to enjoy the sheer joy of a dewdrop hanging from its tip in the mornings. Moreover, I have no business to temper with it when even the monkeys have spared it so far. They just pluck away the unripe little banana fingers unfolding on the upper part.

The purple pendulum of the banana blossom looks a nutritious heart-shaped tree chandelier. Dew drips down during the misty nights. The green little fingers above get into a sturdy claw. Many varieties of sucklers have a nice party during the day including mosquitoes, fruit flies, stinging wasps and the purple sunbird couple that is almost a full-term resident of the little garden. At dusks, a flying fox comes toed by smaller bats at night.

The night falls across a smoggy dusk. The evening twilight and a half moon doing justice to both the night and the day. It seems there is blood on the moon's pale face, a kind of portrait of the bleeding nature. The reddish moon casts glum shadows across the smog. The smog is a regular affair now even in the villages during early winters.

But the worlds, big and small, have to lumber on. A caterpillar has lost its grater, the last bulbous part. It goes like a funny little tractor whose backside mudguards have been taken off. It walks pretty briskly, just that it topples over repeatedly after losing its anatomical symmetry. Accidents abound at this level of existence. But I think it's better than getting crushed altogether. It has had a long day on the floor, doing all these antics, toppling over, lying calmly like a corpse for some time, an ant or two coming to check about the chance of a meal, and there it hops up again to keep claiming its right to life.

A butterfly going for the last sips of nectar before calling for the day. A slumberous darkling beetle and an agile ant bump into each other. The day going for rest and the night getting up for its shadowy tasks. And above all the fears and insecurities, mother nature still trying to assuage the restless, aggrieved child:

'Let me provide warmth for your frozen hands. Let me smile to soak your tears. Let me hold a flower for you to smell and smile. Let me hold light for your eyes even in the dark.'

ᐰᐰᐰ

There is a monitor lizard in the neighborhood. There are little clumps of trees, grass and bushy plants to allow the reptiles maintain a foothold in the rapidly urbanizing landscape. The monitor lizard hatchlings resemble *ghavera*, *vishphoda*, a poisonous reptile in the lizard family, so people run to kill them. Card-playing idlers are at the forefront of this assault. It gives them a break from the mind-sapping focus in the card game.

Sometimes, a group of four or five ducks goes sullenly over the village. They already look like an extinct species because there aren't any waterbodies to sustain their winter sojourn here in the plains. During good old days, the village pond rippled with their fluttering feathers and boisterous quacks. There was even a group of geese in the village pond. They appeared very peaceful and confident but at a spur of some tricky moment, they let loose a round of bassy quacking and seemed very angry. The dogs had their scary tales to share how angry these Donald ducks could become. The sturdy big ducks taught the dogs many lessons in good behavior. By the way, I remember clearly, they slept on one leg and turned their neck backwards to put it on the back for a soft feathery pillow.

The surrounding countryside is under intense agriculture, leaving hardly anything for the migratory winter birds from the Himalayas. To keep the hopes alive for the winged visitors, three white-necked storks still visit the countryside around the village. They have been visiting for the last many years, spending their time with hesitant little flights, measuring the vanishing wilderness with their long strides. They are always together. All three of them cannot be females because they would have gossiped to animosity by this time. They cannot be males also because they would have fought over females and fallen apart. It's either a female with two males (polyandrous stork system) or a male with two females (polygamy, which seems more likely given the scourge of male chauvinism across species).

ᐅᐅᐅ

Those were very simple but careful days. People had their names etched on brass, steel and aluminum utensils. The neighbors usually borrowed kitchenware from each other during weddings. So the post-ceremony retrieval of the items required a strong, unquestionable identification mark. They would also get a tattoo of one's name and village on the arms to give a clue to their identity if someone got lost at a fair. I remember a little boy who got lost at Haridwar fair. His misspelled village name got him transported to a far off village in some other state. He was lucky to be delivered finally after the failed attempt to deliver him at the wrong address.

Those were also the days when the milkmen served as paramours to lots of work-beaten and bored peasant women. In the privacy of the barn, the milkmen had the luck to stare at them as they milked the cows or buffalos. Romance bloomed usually, followed by boredom-killing intimacies. In the drudgery of a hard life, it was a handy diversion. In the pre-dawn darkness, inside the barn, there was a good chance that the milkman provided some succor to the work-beaten peasant woman. No wonder, the milkmen tried their best to collect milk from all barns before the day broke. As most of the villagers, the males at least, slept peacefully and the peasant women already in the yoke of domestic chores in the *brahma muhurat*, the milkmen loitered around with a mischievous glee on their faces.

One was Khome Dudhiya. Reddish, thin, his mongoose face always clean shaven, he moved with lots of business in his role of paramour to a few peasant women. His cream-colored shirt and pants were always ironed to notify his hard-edged intent. He bestowed a few allowances to his special friends of the opposite sex. Firstly, he deliberately allowed them to mix water in the milk. He just took long, joyful draughts at *beedis* and pretended not to look as water turned milk. Now this bumper offer was too big to be ignored by the peasant women. It gave them, and still does, an orgasmic sense of relief to mix water to milk. Next, he gave them maybe a rupee extra for per kg milk. And when he was really happy, he would gift them pieces of cotton clothes for sewing *salwar kameez* sets. In this simple way, he kept on ferrying milk in his iron drums on his bicycle. It was a very successful life. It is proven by the fact that he was never thrashed by any of the irate husbands on account of his romantic inclinations.

The younger crop of milkmen, who now supply milk to households in the nearby town, also have their share of fun. While the earlier generation had fun basically with the sellers, the stylish young milkmen of the present times have goody-goody times with the purchasers in the town. Many urban housewives also lead a suffocating life within the confines of four walls. The rotund young milkman, whom they consider to be carrying a bagful of libido because of his milk diet, comes handy to beat the boredom. These young Romeo milkmen, as they ride their bikes carrying milk drums, carry a boyfriendly look as if they are going on a date instead of selling their milk. In comparison to the milkmen of earlier generation, these flunky milk carriers have to follow the reversed equation in one more regard: as a special favor to their love interests, they supply waterless milk at subsidized rates.

ᐺᐺᐺ

Chand is in his early fifties now. He is unmarried and works as a truck driver. He is a simple, unassuming guy. You hardly notice any airs around him. But he has a specialty. Presently, the current generation has lots of social-media ventilated issues to talk about. But if we go two decades back, Chand was a solid topic to be discussed about, especially among the endowment-size crazy youngsters. Without any competition, Chand was, and most probably still is, the best-hung guy in the village. Literally, every male would lose confidence in himself at a mere look at Chand walking dourly.

Chand was childlike in this regard. He never wet his shorts while taking bath, sitting innocently on the tube-well's water tank wall and giving himself a nice scrubbing bath while dozens of eyes stared in awe. And the legend spread. He was almost a poor man but people far higher in social standing gave him respect due to his USP. People joked that the reason he is still unmarried is because no father would put his daughter in trouble.

There was a story of mythical proportions that even nautch girls on the GB road in Delhi refused him service. One tormented woman, who had taken the risk and accepted money, bit him and escaped while it wasn't yet over for him, saying, 'Who wants to be hospitalized for his bloody 100 rupees!' She slapped him very hard and threw his 100-rupee note on his face. After that he was spurned by one and all in the area.

There was a famous *gupt rog vishesagya*, the sexologist, in the town. Dr. Lubhash Chugh's name was scribbled on all walls in the region ranging from temples to schools to private houses. Wherever there was space, he got it painted with his offer of turning docile sheepish males into rampaging horses. That was the only form of advertizing we saw while growing up because he didn't leave an inch of wall space for any other product or service. Apart from this, secondarily though, he claimed to treat venereal diseases also.

He had grown sagely old after decades of groping his fingers among people's groins, gleefully looking for the weak spots. The people joked that he had taken *nayan sukh*, solace for his eyes, of ogling at one million *guptangs*, secret organs. But the old man was at the shock of his life in his eighties. He still loved the art of checking *guptangs*. As fate would have it, Chand got a painful boil on his special thing. It forced him to visit the venerable doctor. The old doctor gasped, gasped for life in fact, as he stared at the thing. His mathematics of male anatomy gone haywire, he gasped for words. 'O my God!' is all he could manage to mutter as he struggled with words. He was lost in thoughts as if his life's philosophy had crashed. Then he suddenly flared up, 'Take him away....go and make it sit down...how dare you insult a doctor by coming with an awakened thing!' the proportions obviously made him think that it was wide awake. 'It's perfectly asleep sir!' Chand said meekly. Then the old sexologist had a careful second look and slumped into his chair as if he had been finally defeated. 'Did anyone ever allow you to even touch herself?' the doctor asked at long last. He had forgotten about the patient's boil. 'That's why I'm almost virgin,' Chand answered stoically. I think the old doctor would have been more than happy to retire after hitting this milestone in his career.

ᑭᑭᑭ

I was once walking on my little legs by the side of the famished pot-holed road passing the village. I was coming back from the fields. A road-roller and an elephant were going side by side on the tattered pot-holed road. Three PWD guys on the road-roller, a bulky iron elephant itself, went with a lumbering muse. The real elephant carried four *sadhus* who maintained the mammoth creature for their mendicant journey. They had exactly the same slow, unmindful pace, none of them willing to overtake the other. Traffic wasn't much during those days. Now and then a bus, truck or tempo would crawl respectfully from front or behind and carefully maneuvered the crossing by taking its tyres below the road on the opposite side.

I walked behind watching the spectacle unfold. Who would mess with a road-roller and an elephant on the road? So the vehicles maintained their distance. The PWD guys and the elephant-riding *sadhus* looked very confident on account of their solid occupancy of the road. They even chatted in a friendly way, going slowly side by side.

The *sadhus* had opium chillums in their hands and the PWD guys got desirous of some free spirits. They requested and it was accepted by the *sadhus* already in free spirits. Two *sadhus* got down with a chillum and got onto the road-roller and the driver enjoyed the smoky bonhomie. The road-roller rolled almost of its free will. The other two PWD guys stood in front of the elephant as it put its trunk under their bums to hoist them on its back and there they enjoyed the inhalations of freedom with the couple of *sadhus* on the elephant. And there I walked behind looking at their merry ways. It was a far gentler world then.

ɓɓɓ

Time is creeping ahead block by little block. It keeps on ticking to set up the colossal canvas of happenings. And commodified into its pawns we are also shifted around bundled with all our inflated myths. Among the gigantic plethora of events, there are little tales of agonies and ecstasies. This one here seems a sad tale. Life seems to carry a timeworn and dilapidated myth despite all the hypothetical, slow-dawning effervescence about it. And death, the colossal figure, snatches raw freshness to its age-old, wrinkled self.

A ladybird seems dead in the water bucket. I bring my fingertip near the drowned little colorful flier. Instantly crossing the vast chasm between life and death, it uses its energy held in reserves and crawls to the hand of the species that has destroyed countless fellow earthlings. I look at its beautiful red wings speckled with little dots. It gives gleaming insights into the vast array of natural colors and self-evolving designs.

I try to put it on the night jasmine flowers but it looks full of gratitude and moves up the finger. Getting it off is a very delicate, and tough, job. I am not aware that someone is watching me very closely. A rockchat has witnessed the rescue operation. It's keenly interested in what I'm doing. Its dull rufous brown color is misleading. It's not that dumb as it seems. Smartly it picks the ladybird and darts away, giving a triumphant *chick-chick* note that carries a wry sense of humor. Probably it thinks that I'm offering the little colorful beetle to it.

It's one of the pair that hops around in the verandah and the yard and the garden ticking out ants, spiders and other little insects. Sometimes they sneak into the room and are very keen to explore the cage of we humans. They survey the room from the ceiling fan and their dark little eyes seem lost in the encyclopedic fog spread by our hopes and desires. I would say it's a very inquisitive pair of birds and they want to know more about me. Once, one of them, boy or the girl I'm not sure, sat on my writing pad and very comfortably and assuredly eased down a drop on it. Maybe it gave me an autograph.

Sometimes, the rufous brown Indian rockchat is mistaken as female Indian robin, but it lacks the reddish vent and is slightly larger in size than the robin and carries a slightly curved slender beak. It flies like thrushes and redstarts and loves to hop and fly around human habitations. No wonder they have laid claim to the house. They slowly raise their tails as they take little jumps on the ground while picking their feed. They help this lazy countryside writer in keeping a check on the spiders in the verandah. Sometimes they come out even at night when there are moths around the bulb. The pair, quite unlike their unassuming dull color, has a vast repertoire of calls including territorial calls, begging calls, feeding calls, distress calls and roosting calls. But the usual call is a short whistling *chee* delivered with a rapid bob and stretch. Sometimes, they give company to the tailorbirds with their alarm calls, which is a harsh *chek-chek*. And when they are very happy after a nice lunch, they sing like thrush in their moderate, few-numbered notes. They are naughty sometimes and try to imitate the sound of other birds.

The honey buzzer got greedy and regularly flew down for three consecutive days. Now the bees aren't just there to go flying around and gather honey for it. They left the site in irritation. You have to take away only that much as it won't spoil the game altogether. Sadly, now my little garden looks incomplete without the bees. The flowers will miss them. Hope the tiny winged visitors won't forget the garden and will come back some fine sunny day to get pollen for their honey and more flowery smiles for the plants.

A little rodent moves quite cluelessly in the flowerbed. Is it a shrew or mole rat? I'm not expert enough to know the difference. To a layman's eye, there is hardly any difference between the two. I wish it to be a mole rat because they say it brings luck. What is the harm in wishing oneself a bit of luck? These are hard times after all. It's twilight and a bluejay (Indian roller or *neelkanth*) suddenly swoops down from the *neem* branch, where it was sitting stoically for the last half an hour, and takes off a gecko from the compound wall. The gecko will have a nice flight till its carrier lands. Stay indoors you wall lizards if you don't enjoy flying in the twilight.

4

It's quite tough to be a non-drinking member of a wedding party in Haryana. Everyone is drunk to be in an enlightened dimension, leaving me the poor earthling struggling with the ground realities. Since truth is decided by the majority, I feel myself clueless and almost an idiot. The marriage DJ starts blaring. The massive woofers and speakers of the music system shake the ground under my steady feet. The liquor-lovers look more sure-footed with their unsteady feet on a shaky ground. The loud blasts of music leave my ribs shaken.

Drunk peasants give a fantastic thrust to their spirits. They challenge all norms of established mindsets, cultural matrix and constitutional niceties. It's madly adventurous to be among them, I tell you. If you aren't a fellow seminarist to them, then be prepared for an onslaught by the agents of anarchy.

Hinduism is indeed very liberal. The starting song is a dedication to drunkenness. 'Bhola takes a bucket of bhang and shakes his bum to ecstatic dance' is the approximate translation of the rowdy Haryanvi song about Lord Shiva's fondness for bhang. They are so happy that the Lord Himself loves drinking. Dozens of liquor-lovers turn ecstatic.

Flying drones is prohibited without authorization in India. And so is celebratory firing. But most of what we do in celebration falls on the other side of law. A young man is flying a drone to make it the best marriage party ever to have visited the village. Another is firing angry vollies of bullets into the body of a helpless sky. I try to add value to their fun. 'A drone just hovering around is no fun and so is the blind and aimless firing into the sky,' I call their attention. 'You try your aiming skills at the drone,' I propose the scheme to the gun wielder. 'You prove your expertise in flying by taking it away from the bombardment,' I suggest to the drone flier. Dozens of voices grab the option and they are egged on to start the game. Even random, close-eyed shots would have a better chance. The boozed man's careful shot shakes the skies. An electric wire finds the aim. Snap goes the wire with a bang. The scared drone crashes on an attic, making it a perfect drone attack.

There is a spin-off from the same wedding. I come home at night, hugely relieved to come in one piece. But someone bangs fists at the iron gate. He is a most distant relative, so distant that you lose the trail of the relationship if you try to go to the source, who has come attending the same marriage function. He is curtly denied entry into any of the houses he thought had a duty to entertain his stay. Perhaps someone suggested that the writer is a good option under the circumstances. So here he comes to my place. He is unsteady in gait but very steadily holds his feeble right to stay at my place. What will you do, if even after you declaring his totally unwelcome status through your gruff behavior, he pretends to be most at ease as if flowers have just been sprinkled over him, making him the most esteemed guest on earth? You have to be an out and out rascal in bad behavior to help him accept his unwelcome status. The roughest cut-sharp notes are simply songs of welcome to him, so here he is sprawled comfortably on the bed and I take my bedding on a cot in a corner in another room. But before that he prefers to be more welcomed through talks. He is very proud about his vast travels. 'How many places you have visited in India?' I am finally forced to ask, getting curious about his far and wide travels. 'I have travelled far and wide!' he declares. Then he enlists a thorough sketch of his forced entries into the houses in the neighboring districts within a diameter of 50 km. 'I have travelled a lot,' he declares with the world-weary finality of a traveler who has just returned after taking a trip around the earth or maybe even beyond. Thank God, this feeling of world-hopping travel got him sleepy and he dozed off.

But well into the depths of night, another liquor-lover is singing his bawdy songs against humanity. He has drunk away his land and domestic peace. The last installment of the compensation money for his land acquired for a new road project was swiftly drunk away. All that was left was a lakh of rupees. A smart guy cleverly branded his old car at 1.25 lakh rupees. The real price must be around 75000 rupees. He gave a discount of 35000 and sold the car for 90000 rupees. The liquor-lover hits the ceiling in hitting the jackpot.

In return of the favor done to the purchaser, the seller gets a promise to use the vehicle as and when needed till he gets a new car himself. It will be an exception though, he promised to the new owner of the dented old car. In addition, there was another condition. This one made the liquor-lover really happy. He had to promise to take the old owner and his group on two trips to Haridwar. Fun trips, they promised. The two proposed trips to the pilgrimage town saw the rest of the money going out of the pocket.

The borrowing of the car turned out to be a generality, not the exception as promised earlier. There is no new car purchased by the previous owner so far. The frequent borrowings result in repeated tiffs between the neighbors. And carrying the momentum from one of the numerous tiffs, he is now tearing apart the shrouds of dark night with his piercing shouts.

ᗡᗡᗡ

A bluejay or Indian roller (*neelkanth*) sits silently on the top branch of a dead *neem* tree. Dry, dead trees are nice perch points for birds because they can have an unrestricted view of the surroundings. A brooding fellow it seems, a silent bird with stagnant emotions right in the middle of some breezy, fluid moments floating around its beautiful navy blue and reddish brown colors. Then suddenly breaking its scholastic insights, it gives a vocal blast as it takes off yelling *pakrr-pakrr-pakrr*. The resounding warning startles almost all the birds around. Maybe it finds the morning too boring and decides to ruffle a few feathers. The pair of hummingbirds that is enjoying on the marigolds, which seems a novelty in taste because I haven't seen them feasting on the marigolds before this, also shoots off for cover among leafy canopies.

Marigolds, the sturdy, unassuming flowers that keep their smiles for weeks. I have seen honeybees taking a siesta under the warm afternoon sunrays on the marigolds.

A *Parijat* branch hangs low. Whenever I pass under the tree, it touches the crown of my head. I feel blessed. When a tree's branch braces against you, take a pause and feel the touch. The tree is extending its hand to greet you, bless you, touch you to heal. We just need to accept it.

I missed it to tell you before. There was only one rockchat in the house to begin with. It spent considerable time in the garden, yard and the verandah, and sometimes in the room itself. It shared my solitude with an equal right to the house. It looked a lonely bird that seemed to somehow feel the solitudional vibes emanating from the house. Then one fine day it had a partner. In this species both the sexes look the same, so I would take the liberty of christening its gender as per my convenience. I would say he is a boy of the house who has wooed a lady after having a feeling of getting well settled in the house. Now both of them are very happy together. All of us are looking for a touch of solace through companionship. Now they are spirited enough to enjoy their playful supper till dusk. The mosquitoes are flummoxed by a sudden dive in temperature. They keep knocking at the window panes and door wire-mesh. The rockchat couple nicely jumps around to take airy morsels. The littlest inconvenience is that now I cannot make out which one is the boy who got his partner here.

The skies have a treat. A group of eleven ducks goes quacking in V-formation. These sights are vanishing. There is no free waterbody in the village now. I saw thousands in the village during childhood. The village pond is engaged for fishing. It's almost a little lake but they have spun a wire netting over the entire area to deny entry to the visitors from the Himalayas. Imagine a world where the ducks are denied entry to swim. The fish swim, of course. But only till the net is cast.

Quite miraculously, the banana cone is still there after many weeks. Its deep maroon leaves peel off very slowly to the tug of dew and mist. It's lucky to be still there because there are monkeys in the village. The bully alpha rhesus male faces a challenge. There are many lithe, adolescent heroes who are lustily eying his harem. He carries a big scar on his right shoulder and seems to have lost confidence apart from the prettiest female with whom he loitered around with much majesty, pride and big-time pomp and show as his queen consort. The young swashbucklers have surely lured her away. Well, she is within her rights to choose the prince of her heart. This morning the beaten king was seen with the tailless old queen. He had forgotten her altogether. But now she provides succor to his bruised soul. Earlier he would turn back and challenge we humans right on the spot. Today he simply showed his beaten bum and screeched a bare-toothed abuse from a safe distance. Times change. Nothing is permanent. But he has already crammed the village with his pedigree and this thought should give him some solace.

We match the monkeys in more ways than one. We mess things around—ironically even when we suppose we are organizing things, we are in fact sowing the seeds of more disorder and chaos later on. Our gallant spirit has seen us launching 8400 tons of objects into earth's orbit. Our space-conquering spirits have seen us catapulting 25000 objects into earth's orbit. As a result, there is a huge amount of junk that is floating in space. The future spacecrafts and satellites will need decluttering of space. So we will have space *kabaris*. The trash pickers can take pride in their profession now. It will be much esteemed in the coming decades. Your trash is someone's treasure, very aptly said. But we are mindlessly turning mother earth's treasures into piles of trash.

I light a *diya* a dusk. It's a beautiful, little beacon of faith that lights my path into the dark folds of night. The next day the clay *diya* has a left out cotton swab of the wick. I put it in the flowerbed. There are a few tailorbird couples. Cotton is the basic building block of their nest made by sewing three leaves together. They are nice, skilled chaps and expertly stitch leaves to make a nesting cup. I think to be a great human tailor, it must be mandatory to be a diligent tailorbird in the previous birth.

It's mid November. Gone are the pure mists. We now have the metallic haze, the smog. It kills slowly. Right now it burns the eyes and gives the throat an itch. But the birds still have their morning songs and that is an assurance for the time being. We have to believe in nature to save us like it has done so far.

During the winters, the entire Delhi NCR, covering many districts in the neighboring states apart from the national capital, gets shrouded under smog. Stubble burning by Punjab farmers is generally blamed for Delhi's smog. If Punjab fires are majorly responsible for the winter fog in Delhi, then Chandigarh should be equally polluted in November but it stays almost unaffected. Stubble burning is just one of the factors and that too temporary. The political class passes the buck onto poor farmers every year and keeps ignoring the long-lasting issues that make Delhi a gas chamber throughout the year.

꒷꒷꒷

My father demanded peace. New clothes, with their authoritative tautness and showy bickering, pinched his skin, burdened his bones and ruffled his philosophical demeanor. 'New clothes are very hard on the skin. They put a kind of weight on you,' he would complain. 'They pinch and intimidate you,' he would add. So the new set of clothes would go into watery deluge for three or four days to beat out their pinch, showmanship and gimmickry.

As the clothes would wear down with usage and mellow down to old age softness under the rigorous scrutiny of hundreds of washings, he would get in groove with them, finally accepting their presence in sync with the repose inside. 'The only problem is that when a pair of clothes is really worth wearing in softness, it's the time to discard it,' he complained. My mother and sisters won't allow him to feel at his best and go decked up in extremely soft, read it tattered, *kurta-pyjama* just because he found them suitably soft and non-pinchy.

Pa loved smoking, first huge cigars during dandy youth, cigarettes in the slowing-down middle age and coming to a chain-smoking spree of *beedis* in the later part of life. But ganja was a strict no. Once while visiting Rishikesh, he got inspired to taste the unfamiliar substance. An old *sadhu* was taking majestic draughts at his ganja-filled chillum. Pa followed as a well-obliging newly hatched disciple. Then standing at Ram Jhoola swaying over the watery sprawl of Ma Ganga and a cold wind buffeting down the valley, he saw philosopher Plato walking over the Ganges waters. Many will term it as hallucination. But to me these are the realities belonging to a different dimension. Pa loved the works of ancient philosophers and had thoroughly read Plato's works. So maybe Plato decided to give him a *darshan*, albeit when Pa was a bit tipsy on the swinging bridge.

Father felt it best when he visited Rishikesh. 'I feel it so light in my being when I'm there,' he told us. Once Father returns from his Rishikesh trip. The bag isn't yet on the floor before he tells the biggest news spinning out of his time by the Ganges. 'Elephants would have eaten us!' he reads out the scary news. Maybe still under shock because elephants don't eat humans, they trample them. 'Oh did they attack you?' Ma is concerned. We prepare ourselves to listen to the hair-raising episode. 'Yea, very near to that!' Father builds up the momentum of the scary news. 'How?' Mother is serious. 'We were going in the forest and there we come across them!' Father stops as if still haunted by the biggest land animals on earth. 'How many?' Mother wants to judge the scale of danger on the numerical ladder. 'Well, must be a big party because there were many heaps of dung on the path. We were saved just by a whisker!' Father's eyes are wide open with fear. 'You guys got scared of the elephant dung,' Mother laughs in her simple ways of a hardworking woman. Pa is irritated, 'They were just couple of minutes away because the dung was still steaming.' It was winter and fresh elephant poop let out vapors as a proof of its freshness and hence the just recent presence of the elephants. Mother has to accept the gravity of the danger. 'What did you people do?' she asks innocently. 'We took a U turn and tried to run to the capacity of our lungs and legs,' Father seems tired like he has been running all the way from Rishikesh to our village.

ᖚᖚᖚ

Carried by our savage, irrepressible optimism, and the gutsy tradition to progress at any cost, our footprints now crisscross every inch of earth. Our penetrating feudalism now lords over the entire planet, forcing down the rest of the species into subjugation and slavery. With shrinking hearts and broadening brains, we are evolving grotesquely with our supra-physical desires and experimental mysticism. Stuffed into a definitive mindset, we sing the eulogies of human spirit in a monochromatic tone.

Open spaces are losing their relevance. The riveting drama is making us more and more insecure. There are lavish designs and props for the interiors. We feel uncomfortable with open skies and untamed wilderness. The gardens and yards are vanishing and so are the flowers. I'm but happy that my humble house is primarily decorated with the little garden and the unkempt yard. It's a little world but sufficient to host a love-struck purple sunbird couple. They flit around spurred by their exulting, soaring emotions. After taking nectar from the flowers, they let out a full-throated musical ecstasy comprising duets, chorus or even an orchestra. I see them daily as they fly around in their little world. Their joy pervades the air with incorruptible lucidity.

A big party of brown house sparrows goes darting across the smog-blotted sky. It's an assurance that, despite all the telltale signs of natural imbalance, there is still hope because the birds still fly and sing their songs amidst the taunting and tantalizing smog. We have hope till there are free birds singing joyfully.

There is an old dog in the locality. She has all the age-related issues including itching that hasn't left a single hair on her body. We gave an injection. It helped her and she lumbered back from the door of death or deliverance. The fur is coming back. But maybe she has terrible pain somewhere and piteously whines at regular intervals. A puppy gives her ample company and howls to the histrionic capacity of his little lungs. He is learning the art of howling pretty nicely. When he lets loose his symphony, you get anxious as if the doomsday is coming. In any case, he seems a nice companion to the old dog in pain.

The kittens are handsome cats now. They spend most of the time in hunting for rats and female affection. They aren't interested in purring around legs for measly human dole-outs. They carry a selecting and scrutinizing air around them. But they still remember the milk bowl as I find them sitting near it as I step out of the room in the morning. That's my first sight of the day. They mew loudly as if blaming me for getting up late. They vanish for the day after taking their little share of milk. It's a big world to explore, after all.

As I have said, there has been a proletarian revolution in the simian society. The band of lithe, cunning young monkeys has taken away the prettiest females from the ex-king's harem, including the handsome most, curvy-limbed gal, his favorite. He has now the tail-less old crone to lick his scars. As a bruised scholar and beaten strategist, he is learning good manners now. I saw him taking lice off the funny coat of his tail-less old queen. He has to pamper her now; otherwise, she will also ditch him. Now I can understand how it must feel to lose one's kingdom. His attitudinizing airs are gone. It's a pretty methodical development as he doesn't growl and threaten like earlier. Buckling under the episodic treatment of ill-favoring times, he just walks away sadly. Acceptance of the inevitable change is a good thing. But there are too many male monkeys, many of them sired by him only, and one of them will surely take away his old queen as well. It's a narrative of love, lust, cruelty and revenge. Not willing to court any controversy, and far away from the burst of defiance and exuberant idiosyncrasies, his male callousness severally blunted, he seems sexually handicapped, all sedate and subdued. Life is all about farcical reversals. Now the elegant social capital—with its balls, music, gambling and reception—lies in the coffers of the younger generation.

ᖯᖯᖯ

Ballu is around 47 years in age but he is a proud grandfather for the last few years. That entitles him to leave an impressive heritage. The pangs of poverty make one petulant and self-serving. On the dirt-paths of survival, one becomes ever-perky and anxious. The frozen cluster of 'need' is unyielding in its grip. As a poor man liquor comes handy with its promise of unconditional surrender. He is no exception.

But childhood is all about ecstatic swings between dreams and reality. As a boy he loved horses. He galloped like a horse and made whining and neighing sounds of a horse even while we played monkey games. He was also far ahead of his times. At a time when any thought beyond cleaning oneself after ablutions with water seemed like shaking the foundations of the established religion, he cleaned himself Western style. Just that he had a green patch of grass to rub himself clean instead of the toilet paper.

This was a very nice little round patch of grass where we, saturated with childhood satisfaction, rolled in fun. We found it highly objectionable that he should use his ultra-modern style at that place. As a token of self-esteem, we plotted a scheme. We would fix acacia thorns, like booby traps, in the grass to wound the enemy. But luck was with him and we always missed the mark as his habit of continuous experimentation of seeking fresher grass for his rubbing fun saw him choosing the not-booby-trapped areas.

He came to know of the plot and knew that I was the ringleader. Naturally, he counter-plotted. He invited me to ride their old horse, saying it was the most docile creature on earth and hence would just tread at a snail's pace, giving me the pleasure and fun of life. I enjoyed the slow ride, a kind of nice music with one note gracefully beckoning the next one with each step of the horse. Ballu then kicked the horse with full force from behind. The offended creature gave a sudden spurt and took to the capacity of its old legs. There was no bridle or saddle. I was holding just the cord of the neck-bell. As I perilously bounced on the back of the trotting animal, I slipped down to the neck and the human-garlanded horse went pretty fast. Thank God it felt thirsty and stopped by the pond and inclined its neck to drink water. I allowed myself to be dropped into the water like a little frog.

As we are talking of horses, mentioning another episode from those bucolic days won't be out of place. Paltu Potmaker had a fine mare. Young Taqdir Singh had a penchant for horse riding. After grazing at the public lands around the village, the light-footed mare would return lumbering and tired instead of coming out fresh after grazing. It was an invasive trauma to the owner as he came to know about the adolescent boy's fun rides on his mare.

Paltu was a startingly simple man, shy and self-effacing. But he felt offended in this matter. One day, Paltu was returning after relieving himself by the village pond. He carried his empty brass *lota* with him. Taqdir came full gallop raising dust on the majestic mare. In groove with the subtlest sense of time, Paltu gave the best shot of his life. Perfectly aimed. Paltu threw the brass utensil at the rider as he passed him on the path. The potmaker instantly proved that he had all the traits of a great marksman. He hit the rider on the forehead. Taqdir rolled over and fell in the sand on the path. The cut mark on his forehead continued to tell the fact that he was a once fine horse rider.

ᗡᗡᗡ

Happy to be in his nineties, he would be still happier if he hits a century. He loves cricket and he knows the joy of hitting a ton and also the agony of getting out in nineties. He worked in the fields till a few years back and when his body could no longer keep up with his farming zeal, he tried his best to stay at the helm of the affairs and would lumber up to the fields and shout instructions at his son and daughter-in-law to do the chores properly. But even his vigilant overseer's eyes failed him and his enthusiasm dimmed with the fading lights in his eyes. He now spends most of his time at home.

Well, farming has been his religion and agricultural tools his religious idols. His ears have also stopped keeping up with his enthusiasm to eavesdrop on what is going around. But his tongue is thankfully still prompt and spiffy. With all this background, *Tau* Hoshiyar Singh has his farmer's version of Ramayan. We are talking about Lanka. 'It was built by that *devta* who is often seen with his wife,' he enlightens me on the subject. He means the God who is depicted with his wife in the pictures. 'What name is that?' he is asking his better knowing self slumbering in the subconscious chambers of his brain.

The problem is that lot many *devtas* are seen with their wives. We name a few trying to match what he has in mind but he clucks his tongue in a strong no. He then gives a clue. 'It's the one who has that snake around his neck,' he hits the jackpot. 'OK, you mean Bhagwan Bholenath!' we chorus. 'Yea, that's him. He made Lanka but Ravana being a clever devotee and Bholenath being very simple, the city of gold was grabbed by Ravana as a reward for his penance,' the story behind Lanka unfolds.

He has something to share about the masons and bricklayers also. 'Lanka was made of gold bricks. Bholenath told the masons that the little pieces of bricks left out during the construction will be theirs as a reward. The workers but got greedy and would break far-far more pieces than required in order to increase their takeaway. In fact, they broke more than what was used in the walls. The angry God then punished them, "You guys will remain broken in economic means just like bits and pieces you have broken here!" So the masons and bricklayers are poor people. They keep on breaking bricks and however hard they may try they stay as poor as earlier.' By the end of this narration, he felt sleepy and pulled over the sheet over his face and very soon we heard nice rhythmic snoring, giving enough clue to his bright chances of scoring a century of years on earth.

᭡᭡᭡

Most of us are running after a job, car, house, man or woman under the belief that after achieving this we will become happy and joyful. The mirage keeps shifting and the misery of life follows us to the grave. Rashe but isn't trapped in this game. I offer him two quarters of liquor for a small errand, a very small task in nature. He isn't interested. I offer the option of giving the reward now itself with the additional choice of him carrying out the task later, at a time of his choice in fact. It doesn't change anything. The fact is that he doesn't require the thing today and taking the trouble of hoarding something for tomorrow isn't in his dictionary.

Today his friend's friend has a little function. Rashe's friend will surely take him along. So why bother about a thing that is of no use today. I envy the stability of his mind. On the other hand, here we are the lesser fellows cowering under weightier issues, and forced on a precarious walk on a rope drawn between the poles of madness and genius. The walk is so heavy with the baggage of sizzling assumptions on the path of intellectual adventures. In a way, we are plagued with the fear of our own ideas. While he goes slowly and simplistically, moving like an elephant, coolly digesting all the melodrama around.

ⵞⵞⵞ

Those are the days stashed away in a dusty closet. But they hark my attention sometimes to those times of lovely sweet-nothings. The schools of the eighties of the past century in the villages appear like at the other end of the planet in the literary queue. These are fiercely creative and competitive times, unsparingly pushing us into the grip of selfish subjectivity. Modern education seems a savage downpour upon little heads.

But as students at a village school in the eighties, ours was a totally different world. Seeped in the sublimity of simple emotions, untouched by frustrated aspirations, we had all the time to be lazy within the premises, as if recuperating to go all agog after the school. We were all very lazy at the village school. The students and the teachers competed against each other in being relaxed and at peace with one's being. The only time when the teachers showed some agility and quickness was while thrashing and shouting abuses with a cool nonchalance.

The students, in turn, were extra agile in evading anything distantly related to the studies. Laziness would get into an enchanting bloom during the winters. The winters would arrive with limitless grace to bestow the balmy days under the open sun for all of us to dose like a sunbathing python after a hearty meal.

It was a small world and the expectations weren't high. In fact, there was hardly any expectation from almost all the students. As the temperature dipped, the main priority shifted to get extra Vitamin D. The classes would shift to the huge playground. Heavy on brunch, the teachers dozed on their chairs. They would bang the stick on the ground once in a while, throw some harsh word—they were very charismatic and ingenious in their favorite cuss words—and after the temporary fit of anger would again get cool under the warm sunrays.

We would also go into automation mode—like a drowsy cow mulching fodder with eyes closed. We munched upon the dry grass. We chewed a lot of it during the long-drawn days, waiting for the sun to cross the horizon. Doing *jugali* like a buffalo is a kind of meditative practice. It takes you beyond the hard edges of time. Time passes off without too much of a burden. The birds sang in the trees with a virtuous acclaim. And we would lose a bit of that poise only during the last period as we waited for the last bell to go active again the moment it was heard and go hopping for an active evening spurred by a voracious variety of childhood antics.

ϷϷϷ

The game of life and death is admirably enigmatic and stays as big a mystery as it ever was. The eldest woman in our locality is still going perkily to get her old age pension. A decade back her pulse was gone. It wasn't tragic and scary for her family as one isn't too serious about old people these days. She was very old even then. The only issue was that her daughter's fire ceremony in marriage was just minutes away when she stopped breathing. The marriage function was irreversible at that stage.

A new beginning at the threshold and an old chapter closing. It made the situation a bit tricky for the family.

A NOBODY'S NOTEBOOK

So they shifted the corpse to an inner room without announcing the news of her demise to the public. The marriage ceremony was happily completed. The girl was seen off to go to her in-laws' place. Then they decided to check on the corpse. They found her awake and in proper senses. 'Why did you put me in the room, I couldn't see the *pheras* of my granddaughter?' she muffled her complain. 'But you were surely dead!' they exclaimed. 'Yes, I was gone to a distant place but the big mustached fellow yelled, "It's not your time yet, why are you here?" and they pushed me back.'

Well, a few people have shared a similar experience during their near-death experiences. But it remains a big mystery. Usually we take them as hallucinations of a brain struggling to survive. But I'm open to the idea that there may be more to the issue beyond the scientific explanations.

ᗞᗞᗞ

The early winter of mid-November carries a sort of primeval magic and brings vanloads of smiles to the little garden. With its soft brush, the early winter seeks to iron out the flaws and wrinkles in our tangled fates. Everything seems fresh as if holding onto some newfound belief. There is a joyous yearning to bloom and expand.

The scarlet, yellow and orange marigolds are dew-bathed. They are unpretentious and decent in colors and soft in smell. They don't lead an extravagant life and are the octogenarians of the flower world.

The festive spirit seeps into the Jesus thorn. The sorrowful writhings of its prickly stem take a backseat as its red flowers take the front seat in a modest show of flowery pageantry. It's simple button-like flower with two dull red petals twirled around with a yellow centre. A kind of Taoist symbol of the merging duality. It's aptly named—thorns on the stem and the Lord's smile winning over the thorns.

The yellow English rose is shapely and attractive. It's a hardy flower and stays for a few days. But there is no smell in it. The flowery soul is missing in the flowers that have no smell and look good only. The *desi gulab* is redolent with fragrance. It's soft and malleable; its petals scatter without pain and sprinkle their perfumed existence on mother earth like in homage. The smell-less hardy English rose stays for a longer time. A kind of over-attachment. It turns into a piteous corpse while still clinging to the branch. It wants to retain its beauty. The petals start decaying making it ugly after a time.

Coleus (*mukundi* or *pather choor*) appears to be an illuminating and intuitive plant. It has heart-shaped scarlet leaves with green frills around the edges. Its leaf itself seems a flower because it's decorated as such. It's said to cure many diseases ranging from cholera to cancer.

Did the honeybees go away for a few days to dupe the honey buzzard because he got greedy and started coming daily? They have returned now. It's a bigger ball. Probably they allied with another little group of lost bees and formed a bigger one. This time they have chosen a strategically more secure branch on the curry-leaf tree. Late November has many flowers in my small garden and they need not go too far to collect pollen for honey. As I stand in the garden, a delicate fragrance of wild honey wafts around me. It's better to have little winged visitors who go dancing on the flowers. It keeps your hopes alive if you have the delicate smell of honey wafting around you.

The birds also feel better. You can make it out from their songs. Asian pied starlings are very gossipy. They always land on a tree in a little group and are always very excited and talkative. They seem to have a lot of things to chatter about. But somehow they don't seem bitchy.

The main advantage of having cats in the garden is that the squirrels stay away. They are great at stealing eggs, especially the eggs of scaled munias. The rufous little bird with a black and white checker-work on its breast is not quarrelsome. Their notes sound sweet even when they are angry. The nest is high on the branch where the cats cannot reach. So it looks a likely case of successful hatching this time.

These are hard times. To attract love one has to make a lot of noise and be at one's showy best. The little guy, the purple sunbird, is in a flurry. He is excited to get some love. The *Parijat* trees have started to retain their flowers to make seeds as December approaches. The sun is emerging above the mist with its minute-by-minute evolving compassion to give warmth after a chilly night. The little bird takes a sip of the dew-laden white blossom. It then hops around in excitement, showing exquisite energy through its flitting and flashing maneuvers. It slightly twitches its tail and shakes its yellowish underside as the furtive notes of *chik-chik-fich-fich-sich-sich-hitch-hitch* pierce through the air.

Marvelous is the play of passions. Its magnetic appeal makes it both miraculous and mundane at the same time. Love, and oftentimes infatuation, keeps one hostage to the core of its melody. Flying with flamboyance, chirping out its ephemeral emotions, it is calling its partner. I hope she hasn't ditched him for a handsomer bird.

You have to work hard and be serious to retain the love of your lady. Love might be mystifying but there are practical matters to attend as well. It jumps onto the banana cone, a scarlet leaf is unfolding at the upper end, exposing another row of tiny fingers with wispy, hairy ends.

It takes a quick sip from a tiny banana finger and seems sobered a bit. It then gives quieter, sweeter notes of *peek-peek-peek*.

You cannot just call back your lady by being all out aggressive. Aggression is devil driven. It breeds emotional self-destruction. Pain and loss are its selfish sidekicks. You have to be magnificent, primarily with maturity. You have to show your softer side. It now looks a deadly charmer indeed. And there she returns, putting his soul at rest. They are very happy to be together again and go hopping around the neighboring trees.

ᐯᐯᐯ

During our childhood, my brother loved birds, mostly as pets. Flying birds cannot excite a child like they stimulate the poets. He fancied catching a hawk and carry it as his pet. A boy with a hawk surely would go as the undisputed leader of the neighborhood urchins.

Shikra is a relatively smaller bird of prey. The wilderness around the village was yet to be tamed. It meant we had many *shikras* in the sky during those days. The bird hovered in the air—at one point in the sky like a helicopter—as it took aim at some field rat among the bunch-grass, sedge and shrubbery around the village pond.

The majestic hunter caught my brother's fancy. He mustered up his band. They observed that the small hawk suddenly swooped down, literally fell over the rat. There would be a scuffle of few seconds before it took to air again with its take-away. And here the band of boys smelt a chance. They procured a big, wicker-worked fodder basin used to feed cattle. They planned to hide among the bushes and drop the instrument made of mulberry switches and canes over the hunter, while it struggled on the ground to tame its prey.

The thing was thrown hundreds of times over a period of weeks. And finally they had the catch. The cattle feed basin landed on an impressive cluster of bushes. The hawk made a timely escape. As they approached to retrieve their hunting gear, a big black snake hissed from under it. A snake being too much for a pet, they ran away leaving the snake with its nice kennel. An elder person had to go and fetch the thing after the snake had rejected its new home, finding it reeking with cattle saliva and sunlight filtering through the narrow chinks.

5

'The Window' is a beautiful Persian movie. No big efforts at super-heroism, no ironies of heart-breaks, no bombastic romance, no gooseflesh rippling drama, no thunder-stricken rigmarole of saving the planet from the aliens. It's not about chafing thoughts, it's all about the frolicking gaiety of common emotions in the life of common people.

Beyond the grinding millstone of bigger caprices, it's about sublimated emotions. It creeps genteelly like a flowery vine. It's a long-drawn painting of beautiful hills, smatterings of snow on the slopes, chatty streams, green pastures and a sense of virginal peace to tow all these along. There are no chivalric, lionized doctrinaires delving into deep mysteries of human existence. It's a gently flowing painting on a self-absorbed canvas. The human characters simply add to the soft shades of the softly evolving painting.

In his small world, little Ali takes soft, chiming steps to be a nice human being. With a working-man's prudence, he contrives a canvas and paints his simple pictures using pomegranate juice, egg yolk, charcoal and leaf paste. He paints to bring a smile to a girl who is bedridden and cannot come out to play. The old, reclusive painter who teaches him to paint has an unfinished painting by his son who has gone missing.

The missing young man loved portraying virginal, untouched scenes. He has left an unfinished painting of a lone tree on a hilltop against the background of snowy peaks. As a sort of *gurudakshina* for his old painting teacher, little Ali roams around the hills to find the location of the tree in the unfinished painting. He finds the place and this is where the old man comes across the grave of his lost son.

Then the caravan of life takes Ali's family away. Before they move, little Ali gives their small TV set to the sick girl's poor family. She already has started smiling looking at those softly drawn pastures, streams, sunrises and hills painted by Ali. Through his little acts he is learning to paint a real life beautiful picture.

ᕃᕃᕃ

In the pre-dawn silence of a cold morning, a laughing dove sadly coos her dissatisfaction about love. A broken heart that wants to be heard in the eerie silence. A puppy barks. Someone clears his throat loudly. A jungle crow caws. A tailorbird picks up his notes. A shoal of house sparrows sings morning prayers. The day has begun.

This is the first week of December. There are no farm fires now but the air quality index (AQI) in Delhi is still hazardous on the pollution scale. The narrative about the farm fires helps the politicians in hiding their failure year after year. During the winters, the AQI becomes more important than the Sensex. It should nail down the fact that we are now at the edge of a painful fall. Take climate change seriously.

You realize the real worth of sunshine after a few overcast days in the winters. Sunless days in winters stare at you very snappishly. And when the sun shines openly one fine morning, you welcome it with gratitude. It heals you like your frozen hands get a lease of life on a warm hearthstone. You run to put the damp clothes to dry. In my enthusiasm, I hang clothes on the line and block the little aloe vera plant's share of the golden rays. The plant must have complained for I realize the mistake. I remove the hurdle and warm sunrays kiss its green spiky sturdy leaves. Soak your part of the sunrays but take care not to block others' part.

Another little family of honeybees came scouting for a place to pass the winters. They hovered over the little clump of trees in the garden. The resident honeybees must have objected to another hive so nearby. There was a lot of confusion for some 15 minutes, or maybe even some scuffles and heady altercation. The visitors agreed to the objection and settled for the *giloy*-covered acacia clump outside the fence.

The little sapling of *peepal* is doing well in the nursery bag. It was a tiny sapling, dusted, crushed, barely visible among the cracks in the yard bricks. I retrieved it and planted it in a little nursery bag. Bathed it with tiny water droplets and the dust came off its half-crushed little leaves—just three of them. The thin stem was almost mauled. It barely held onto life for two-three weeks, neither dying nor growing. And then one fine day a new leaf shone under the mild winter sun. Let's hope it will be a majestic, massive tree one day.

A blue monkey from the blue dye factory enters the village. It's a small unit a few kilometers from the village on the road to the town. The monkey made its territory there and maybe loved the heady smell of the chemical and the blue-spattered compound. But it lost the red of its face and bum in the bargain. Then getting bored of the monotony there, it left the place and entered the village. The rest of the monkeys are scared of him. He has come seeking company but they run away. I think he better approach the ladies in the dark. He can claim to have descended from the heaven and try to be their King by default for being completely exclusive.

Granduncle's Labrador Tuffy has a gruffy bark now. It seems his throat is overused. Actually, a rascally young monkey sits on a tree overlooking the terrace. He keeps teasing the dog. The latter keeps barking. By this time, there are too many simian residents in the village. Almost every roof has a claimant. It seems there has been mass emigration to the village. They love the concrete jungle. Tiny baby monkeys have nice play-spots on the roofs. They slide down the slanting rooftop solar panels. They are learning to bite properly also. They practice on solar-system cables.

Well, coming to some warmth in the chilly days of December. A cat comes with a lot of warm flattery—if you feed it well—and lots of purring around your legs. But you cannot avoid some extras from the feral cats who pay you visits and get friendly. They arrive with poop as well. Maybe they think they are paying you back for your kindness. It forces you to be more tolerant. Small-time writers can learn to share the sun-bathed terrace with cats. They love sleeping as much as I feel like writing. So I try to draw better inspiration and ignore the drying cakes of cat poop. If you cannot do that then stop pretending to be a writer and be a cat-beater.

פּפּפּ

There are very well educated and well-off beggars as well. Their first instinct is to demand money. Like this gentleman in a BMW on a congested road at the local town. In a messed up bumper-to-bumper situation, a rickshaw-puller gives a tiny bruise to the expensive machine's taillight. The rich beggar gets down, puffing out fumes of anger, and slaps the poor, old, weak rickshaw-puller. And straightaway demands money for the damage. He holds out his hand. He wants money at any cost.

ᛒᛒᛒ

Tau Hoshiyar had a minor stroke at the age of seventy-five. Well, that was more than two decades back. As it struck him and he began losing his senses, the entire street panicked and ran helter-skelter to arrange some means to convey him to the town hospital. But extricating him from the stone pillar was a tough job. He thought he was going to die and getting him to the hospital would mean an economic ruin to his farmer son.

'Don't ruin yourself by taking me to the hospital!' he kept yelling. He had strong limbs so it required the effort of a few people to loosen his grip even in that condition. He lay there as a terribly unhappy man on the hospital bed. I went to meet him at the hospital. Finding me having some semblance of education among the work-brutes, the doctor held out the scans of his brain and explained the situation.

Tau stared very hostilely from his bed. To him, every hour spent in the hospital was a sort of plunder. Before this episode, he hadn't spent even a single night at a hospital in his life.

'Now anything to do with ghee and hookah is a poison and sure death to him!' the doctor told me in a loud voice so that *Tau* would hear the message. *Tau* was very hostile to the doctor, so the gentleman conveyed the message indirectly. *Tau* found it a blasphemy against a farmer. Ghee and hookah are the basics of farming religion. After coming home, to take revenge, he increased the intake of both the forbidden items. Now after more than two decades, and loads of more ghee and hookah, he still goes to the *chaupal* to have a feel of the crowd. Well, human system seems a mystery. Some inner fine-tuning and joy is the wellspring of longevity. I mean staying in wretched mood and proper diet won't do.

I recall an incident when he had come visiting my house once. We were sitting on chairs in the courtyard and gossiping. His teacup arrived. He put it on the ground by the side of the chair for letting it a bit cooled. A fly committed suicide in his tea. He coolly picked up the cup and took out the dead fly. '*Tau*, don't drink it. We will get you another one,' I tried to stop him. But he had his logic hammered on the anvil of a tough farming life. 'You never know, even a fly mixed in hot tea may work like a medicine on one's system. Strange are the ways of God,' he said and drank his tea with much comfort.

Well, I missed to tell about another old *Tau* who was put in a bed by our *Tau's* side at the hospital. He was in his eighties and looked very helpless as if he wanted to run away. I asked his grandson about what happened to the gentleman. 'He had kidney stone pain. Someone told him that drinking limejuice cuts the stone. So he bought five kilos of lemons, wrung out the juice out of the entire stock and mixed it in a bucket of water and drank it within five or six hours. And now here he is!' his grandson told me.

ܦܦܦ

An electric cable goes over the terrace. It dangles pretty low; precipitately close to my nose if I stand by it. It may be risky for my head but it has pleasant undulations for the birds that perch on it and jabber, prattle, babble and chirp. I requested my neighbors to do something about it a few times but they are a joyful family and don't find it a serious issue. After much soul-searching and introspection, I learn from them that it really is not a serious issue. I also learn how to avoid getting a huge dent on one's ego by little pot-shots of trivial issues. It also trains you in how to avoid downcast mood. Further, it's training me in the art of alertness. I have to abandon my insufferably amateurish ways. Ever on the vigil, I duck down very carefully every time I pass through. It's a nice stretching exercise. Further, one monkey in particular loves taking a quick, exhilarating swing on it as it passes over the roof.

Electricity fluctuates quite riskily at nine in the night; it's a kind of sepulchral infraction upon the cold, limpid stream of darkness. Some problem with the lines, yes. It's a monkey doing acrobatics, enjoying some mysterious cerebral delirium, on the electricity pole. They carry mammoth intrepidity in aerial acrobatics. The winter days are falling short in accommodating their profoundly bashing enthusiasm. They have an incontestable right for fun and frolics. So to compensate for short winter days, they have extended their work-hours into the nights.

By the dint of his special color, the blue-dyed monkey has a woman in his life. Maybe she is just curious or the type who wants an outstanding prince charming and be a part of the local simian folklore. In any case, love-rhymes have a lot of scope for experimentation.

Calmly carried by an inexorable sublimation of wits, the dove seems foolish in addition to being peaceful. Past lessons are of no avail. They are so lazy as if the God owes them amends. The very same little flimsy nest, a little step away from obliteration, and the scene of so many cat and eagle crunchy egg breakfasts and suppers, is again ready for another serving with a look of solicitude. Earlier it was the spotted dove, now it's the turn of a laughing dove, with their delightful keynotes, to come and lay eggs in the house of tragedy. No wonder, the cat is in very good spirits. Lost in cold, warm and tepid dreams, he sleeps under the small curry-leaf tree. Let her lay the eggs, he will climb there as easily as one walks up the steps on a staircase. The doves are plainly lazy. There is hardly any plea in their defense.

Engulfed by the giddy immensity of childhood, little puppies just love barking. The days leavened with just fun and more fun before the chafings, gashes and bruises of growing young and then old take a firm grip on the wheel of life. Last night, this little puppy in the street didn't feel sleepy at all. It led the chorus encored by at least ten to fifteen dogs. The moment they spent their lungpower and stopped to take a breather, the tiny puppy would again come with its lead lines. And the elders would again fall into the chorus. A very busy night in the paroxysm of restlessness. They carried the barking rigmarole well into the wee hours. The lead composer must have slept then, bringing an end to the orchestra.

𝔭𝔭𝔭

The neighborhood *Kaki*, during her youth, came to know of the secret of taming men in a hand-to-hand fight. In verbal assault, she would leave any sense of male chauvinism battered, bruised, bleeding, lacerated, torn, tattered and racked. But over the perilous crossroads of physicality, where the females generally shrink back on the defensive given the animalistic forces residing in the males, she once incidentally found the key to matching them in the raw power game as well.

She was returning from the fields one not so fine dusk. The shades of night loomed large with a much-vaunted singularity. The slack and tardy stretch of the dusty road across the isolated countryside brought an incendiary encroachment upon her dignity. Two men pounced upon her with a very, very wrong intention. Scared to the guts and haunted by the bewildering ramifications of their intention, God graced her with the chance key to save her honor.

To save her *ijjat*, she clung to the very same instrument of their bestiality. She gave a spellbinding squeeze to the both of her peasant woman's strong fists. The attackers were left in a preposterous firmament of pain. The more they howled, the more pressure she applied. *Kaki* proudly dragged them by their weakness into the village.

This exquisite masterpiece left her much spruced up against the so-called physically stronger sex. It gave her huge encouragement to tame down men in family feuds, which were obviously very decent in numbers among the peasant families. Over the coming decades, she became a terror who could hold men from 'there' and after squeezing the life out of the male pride, she would pin them down and gloatingly sat on their chest to claim victory. As little children, we witnessed many of her victories. The rivals discussed the escape strategies and advised each other about keeping the middle part out of her grasp. But how far you will stretch your behind? One cannot keep one's middle safe at home and go to fight. So obviously *Kaki* found her targets.

One particular branch of her extended family specially bore the brunt of her major technique. First the grandfather lost his honor in his dhoti, followed by his son in the *pyjama*, and now the grandchildren in their pants carried the ignominy to the third generation.

Kaki was ageing now and the young fawns wanted revenge. Two of them challenged her at the village pond. *Kaki* groped for her strength and their weakness. She failed in her grasp this time and they walloped her pretty soundly. She was howling with pain as she ran to the village. 'They aren't men! Had they been really men, I would have squeezed them into defeat!' she went crying.

Well, the boys were very smart. They were wearing cricket guard, and below it tight *langots*, which the wrestlers use to guard themselves in close duels, when they challenged her. No wonder she missed the target this time.

ppp

The days have feeble sunrays across the hazy veil of misty noons. The sky looks gaping with stupefaction. And the winter ambling its way through December with a proud nonchalance. There is a pair of oriental white-eyes on the small curry-leaf tree. The tree may look small but it seems to be patronizing a lot of birds apart from the honeybees. There is a pleasant commotion defined by delicious preening chimes of these little green birds having a coquettish white ring around their eyes. Earlier they used to come for nesting in the garden but with the cats around they think better of nesting here anymore. They aren't dumb like the doves.

The *Parijat* flowers now don't drizzle like sad tears with the breaking of dawn and stay during the day as the trees have started to retain them to make seeds to spread their progeny during the next monsoon. Hovering with a keenly searching intensity, the purple sunbird couple goes into a tailspin of ecstasy as they raise a cheepish ruckus. They seem to be enjoying the love-bond to the limits under a delicious dose of sunrays on winter noons.

Outside the yard walls, a honeysuckle has crept high into the foliage of an acacia tree. The clinging shrub has spread its shoots pretty luxuriantly. A group of house sparrows roosts there for the night. When they are sitting together during the noon, they fall into a very heated conversation. Given the seriousness, it must be a very important issue. Did some dandy sparrow have a hit on someone's partner? Then they realize that there are better ways of spending time and energy than peddle into a tug of war over issues related to amorous passions. A communal bath follows in the clay water bowl on top of the wall. The gossipy issue gets sidelined and bountiful play starts.

ᗡᗡᗡ

This particular hawker's selling-call has been an enigma for months. It sounds superposed by inexpugnable traces of secrecy. I simply failed to make out what is his product or service. The drooling notes of insipid loquacity turned troublous enough to niggle at my curiosity. But by the time I would come out to check, he was gone.

In my estimation he could be anything from a trash-picker to a cloth seller. There is a dog in the neighborhood that howls in response to all moods and situations. Its character seems to be interwoven with indissoluble sinews of sadness and misery. Give him the best bone, he will howl painfully as a show of his obligation. Get him engaged to the most beautiful feline girl, he will express his gratitude through an even more piteous howling. In fact, it will howl even while at the top of a weaker dog in a fight. But it would forget its whimpering—eighth wonder—at the sounds of this hawker. Maybe the hawker's speech leaves him confounded.

Then one fine day, I found out the secret. I was standing outside and was lucky to witness his few seconds of hawking spree before he vanished around the corner. It's a vegetable seller pulling his rickshaw cart. There is the feeblest of auditory resemblance to *aaloo, gobhi, matar, pyaj* in a rumbling jumblement of jittery linguistics. I think even a Tahitian coming to the outer world for the first time in his life would do better in his first attempt at pronouncing Hindi words for vegetables.

There he was vanishing on his royal march as if the buyers have the obligation to run after and seek his blessings. I raised my hand and harked from behind. The dog that was having a break in howling to bark instead looked at me and reverted to his howling position as if complaining over something. The vegetable seller was gone without paying heed to my accost. The dog kept howling with its usual finesse.

ᑀᑀᑀ

It was almost like unleashing a tiger on one's own father. This feral cat had this bad habit of littering at all the wrong places in and around our house. It was thus ordained that she was to be taken to stick as and when seen without losing any time.

I saw her sleeping under winter sunrays on the stone slabs overlooking the inner yard. Like a supreme predator, I stealthily picked a bamboo stick and poked at it quite forcefully from the railings above. It received quite a hard poke at its ribs that sent it out of its wits. Not having much clue about what to do, it jumped down in panic.

It was a beautiful day for sunbathing. Father had a close crop of his grey hair and had given a nice oil massage to his scalp that needed attention and pampering after weeks of lying hidden under his woolen cap. The idiotic cat landed straight on his philosopher's head. Well, the cat took revenge for its fall. Father had scratch marks on his scalp. The act turned unpardonable even with the cat's entire set of littering crimes.

'You are good for perpetrating a self-goal only! Why didn't you hit her in a way so that she landed anywhere on earth except my head?' nursing his scratch marks, Father turned serious enough to settle a score from his side.

However, he was a kind man in every sense of the term. The instantaneous flare of anger was curbed, the red flame changed to a grumbling of some words about my foolishness, then to some stoic reflection, followed by some clandula ointment on his injuries. Then a book found him well absorbed in its pages. Father would forget all individual and collective miseries, even if there was a nuclear strike, as long as there was a nice book in his hands.

ᐅᐅᐅ

A sunny winter day and many an old bone wringing their hands in glee for being thawed by gently warm sunrays. There is some noisy, hard-line rhetoric in the clump of trees. Sparrows, babblers, tailorbirds, pied starlings and the rufous treepie couple all raising very serious objections about someone. Dousing hours are shaken awake.

A cat is looking for breakfast, aptly following the trail of passion and pain in the natural scheme of mother existence. The visitor treepies have a dominating freewheeling *chikr-chikr-chikr* verbal pot-shots. All the local birds raise a hot rhetoric and defeat the transgressor. Cobwebs on its face, it comes back with a beaten expression. It then pauses near the latest occupant of the fragile dove nest. She has the patience to wait till the bird of peace is done with laying her eggs. As I have already said many times, the doves are extremely lazy. How do they even survive as a species on the crafty and tumultuous stage of life? It's an incisively dug big question in my mind.

I have a self-styled bird-feed vessel. It's a discarded clay pitcher's mouth-ring. Put it on the wall and it turns a nice little basin to hold millets and grains for the birds. Little groups of sparrows are busy in it through the day. One sparrow loves picking little grains. But she loves scaring others even more. Let a fellow sparrow come near and she would jump and give an angry peck at its fur. When she is around, the rest of them wear a hassled look. Even a balding big male sparrow had to retreat under her chirpy attack. Then there was some noise and all of them scurried away including the quarrelsome one. Why fight with your own pals, especially when there are bigger dangers around?

One of the peacocks has a small plumage having shed its burden. It allows him surplus energy to see more of life beyond the routine obsession about impressing the peahens. It's a free wayfarer now and takes off from one roof to the other in style. Its take off is preceded by a single, steel-straight, short and loud burst using all the vocal chords in its beautiful neck. As it flies to its destination, it goes sailing with shrieking notes of *ayeoo ko-ko-ko-ko*. It's this sound that has scared away the sparrows.

Even with their unassuming dull brown color, the rockchats look at you very intelligently. The rockchat couple is really feeling at home in and around my house. They are a very comforting company for a bachelor struggling writer. Their presence is very unobtrusive. Their dull color won't draw your attention. And despite their chatty name, they are usually very silent as they hop around the yard, garden and the verandah taking little picks of insects from the open platter of mother nature. Driven by curiosity, they give me company inside the rooms as well, as they sit on the ceiling fan and ponder over some strange things. Theirs is indeed a very friendly presence.

ᑭᑭᑭ

Ram Mehar is a robust 77-year-old man. He is visually challenged since birth. A big loss indeed but at the same time he gains a bit, even though it is no compensation, by being spared of the frazzled and faded travesty of the visible life around. He has an almost infallible skill at the rest of his senses minus the sense of seeing.

His main challenge is to stay updated with the changing nooks, corners and bends in the village streets. He has to keep the latest changes in his mind. To recompense him for the loss of light in his eyes, destiny has given him an ability to pronounce Hindi words almost perfectly, which is an oddity among the farmers whose hair-raising linguistic anecdotes give enough proof to the fact that theirs are the tongues especially made for slowly drooling, rumbling, intimidating, abusive sounds in Haryanvi. Chaste Hindi is farthest from the reach of their tongues. Ram Mehar speaks best Hindi in the village.

He has inherited two acres of land in his name. As per local custom and belief, marriage is mandatory to attain *moksha* after death. They got him a purchased bride when he was sixty or a bit more than that. A well-washed, scraped, brushed and dainty Ram Mehar led the marriage party to the poor girl's native place in neighboring Uttar Pradesh. It was a rocking milestone in the empyrean torpor of his many decades on earth. Many farmers enjoyed sweets and cheap liquor. It cost him about one lakh rupees, out of which fifty thousand rupees were paid to the bride's father as purchase money.

Selling girls for marriage in lieu of money is an established profession. The brides usually run away and the agents get them married again to some needy guy. It's a lucrative business. So the bride-buyers keep a strict vigil lest they run away. People had sympathy for blind Ram Mehar, and hence many eyes kept a watch on her. As a result, she couldn't run away.

After two months, she being not able to slip away of her own, her wards arrived to call off the marriage. The villagers demanded the money back. 'What money?' she snapped. 'Only if you guys knew how did I manage! A servant would charge at least twenty thousand rupees for two months. For the rest, don't force me to open my mouth. He is a young rascal "there"!' she pointed at a part in his body. 'His night funs won't come at less than five hundred rupees per night. So that makes it another thirty thousand rupees. That settles it; we don't owe anything to him.'

That indeed settled it as the villagers got impressed with his power and forgot about the main issue. He lost the money but got some new reputation for being very young and strong 'there'. In fact, the people bestowed him more respect after that.

ᐳᐳᐳ

The dove sits perkily on the small, flimsy nest. Two eggs are visible from below as I peep into the nest, precariously perched just a bit more than a couple of feet above my head. The cats have a dependable eyesight I have heard. Let's see when will the cat have his *nasta*.

A *sadhu* comes knocking at the gate asking for alms. He is lucky in receiving twenty rupees over the gate but luckier still in escaping unhurt. The dog that howls only thinks it suitable to taste his calf muscles. Of course, it doesn't growl before the intended bite. But it doesn't howl also. However, he misses it. A tiny scrape of the *sadhu's* loincloth comes in its mouth. The *sadhu* gives a nice strike with his stick. The dog has a sound reason to howl then. But then it barks! The first time I hear it. Well, maybe his is a reversed canine equation.

ᚹᚹᚹ

If you want to hone patience into the fabric of your persona, wait for the day when your kitchen has green fenugreek leaves. Then take your offer to your mother, sister, wife, girlfriend, partner or the maid or whosoever has the task of using the said leaves. Start picking out the leaves from the thin stems. Now, this is a job you simply cannot rush through. It takes it own time.

After a while, the impatience and restlessness in you will settle down to an acceptance that picking one tiny leaf at a time from the fragile stem is an art that is its own master. A calmative sense of patience downs upon you then.

Also, if you want to drill the principles of caution into your attitude, look for an opportunity when the kitchen sink is full of precious but fragile crockery. Offer your services at washing these. You of course need to be very careful because the littlest smudge at any corner lays the entire piece waste. Caution and carefulness in handling valuable crockery will make you learn the importance of carefully handling the modern-day relations that are hundred times more fragile than the crockery set in your kitchen.

ᚹᚹᚹ

The *sadhu's* phantasmagorical strike at the ever-howling dog, the sprightly sniveler, astounded it to the extent that it finally came out of its crying doctrinaires and barked for the first time. So it may be counted as a blessing by the mendicant because a dog without bark is nothing short of perfidy in the canine world. Having abandoned its frightful peculiarity, it docks its tail with a certain swagger. The dog has started barking finally. It's a neighborhood news item.

The best liquor-lover in the locality, who sets up the most loquacious and abusive drama after getting sloshed—having plenteously pawned away most of his possessions—inadvertently struck the dog with his cycle. He was holding his cycle and reversing it. The sleeping dog was hit by the tyre as it rolled over the dog. The dog took it as a breach of honor. It must have felt like a thunder-strike to the sleeping dog because—following the momentum built after the *sadhu* episode—it barked.

It's such a nice change in the street. The barking dogs are far more preferable than the howling ones. Maybe it was waiting for good reasons to bark all this time and the *sadhu* and the liquor-lover finally provided it one. Even though it still finds most of the issues and objects worth howling at only, but its mysterious sufferance gets a few moments of break at the sight of the liquor-lover. The other day, the liquor-lover once again bespattered the street air with his doctrinal cuss words, raising a terrible show with an abominable ravishment. As a few people gathered to shove him back to his house, the dog gave them suitable strength and company by following the party and barking all the while. He followed them and chivalrously barked as if to say, 'Take this idiot to his house!'

By the way, there is a fat black puppy in the street. It was standing by the gate and I suddenly happened to open the gate. The sound startled it so much as if an apocalypse was unfolding. It's an angelic little roly-poly cute thing. Almost a dark ball. A mere look at it will suffuse you with lovingness. Scared out of wits, it showed consummate skills at running. It rolled over its tiny paws and covered majority of the flight in rolling motion.

It reached a safe distance and then barked cutely, showing the embryonary canine sense in its little brain. Well, it inspires me to do the same when against a danger. Running away is a fun. It's brave in fact. You need to be strong to run away from tricky situations and angry people.

ᐅᐅᐅ

A chilly mid-December morning with minimum temperature around six degree celcius. The air seems to carry an enigmatical succor for lonely writers. The cold-beaten trees stand with a pointed disinterestedness. My tea seems to inspire a tiny baby frog. It's safely tenanted for the winters but it sneaks out of the little niche in the plaster in a corner in the verandah. A very courageous feat for a frog to come out in the open in the middle of the winters. Maybe it's very hungry.

It can't hop around, given its frozen blood, it just crawls on all fours. It laboriously crawls around for half an hour. But these aren't the perpetual merrymaking monsoon days. It's a barren field, no ants, flies or mosquitoes. The distance it has covered will come to be at least a mile for a human if we use a comparative scale. There is nothing to eat. Dejected it comes back to its hiding hole. But it reminds me that I haven't taken a long walk in the countryside this winter. Cold is no plea as this tiny frog reminds me. One should be in a position to take inspiration from whatever source it comes from.

The little frog may have gone back hungry but the weaving ants on the tree seem well stocked for the season. Do you know the weaving ants are our predecessors in farming and cattle rearing? They set up their institutions in the form of leafy pans by gluing many leaves in a farmstead unit on a tree. They then gather live aphids in the leafy bowls and rear them pretty considerately. The aphids secrete a kind of sugary drop and the ants milk it as their reward for rearing these aphids. They even give mollifying tickles at the tiny aphids to encourage them to secrete the drop in playfulness. They protect them, feed them well, gently take back the stray aphids that go out like an errant sheep from its shelter. Every ounce of this existence is daubed with natural intelligence. It already exists and it isn't the sole prerogative of the human beings.

At night, the winter moon, even with its auroral radiance, cuts a lonely figure. The villagers sneak into the safety of their rooms just when it gets dark. The trees then share their solitude with the lonely moon. They whisper softly as dew and mist bathes their weather-beaten leaves. The dew crowns the flowers and all of them look happy in the morning, holding some paradisiacal secret in their smiles.

ﭘﭘﭘ

Little Jitender, nicknamed Jitte, had some playing marbles during the eighties of the last century. Those were the days besprinkled with ineffable traces of playfulness looming in the idyllic village air. But a little boy is still a little one, and sometimes even the scintillating and ravishing virginities of childhood fail to beat the boredom. So even with a lot of marbles jingling in his pockets, he felt bored with the usual type of play with the marbles.

Sehdev's buffalo, sitting and chewing cud with incontestable nonchalance, appeared a nice subject for pampering the prodigally tumultuous spirit in the boy. The best-looking big, black marble was now in the buffalo's possession, albeit for a little time, as the buffalo would ease herself and lose it again. From all angles, the deed was too much rough hewn even from the standard of childhood acts of omission and commission.

A rival urchin saw him performing the task that was meant to beat Jitte's boredom. He ran to inform the owner. The farmer, for good reasons, took it as if the honor of his buffalo was violated. He was left fuming with a sense of indigence and anger. Now little Jitte's honor was imperiled. The rough farmer magisterially held the culprit. A bright colored marble glistened in his fingers, itching to settle scores and get justice for his buffalo.

'Now you will realize how it feels to come into the possession of a marble the wrong way!' he gnashed his teeth. But before he could carry out the revenge, Jitte's hefty grandmother stomped both her elbows into the farmer's back, sending him rolling over in the dust. Sehdev himself came dangerously close to feel the experience of his buffalo. It took the effort of a few people to retrieve him with his honor intact. The malevolent marble was snatched from her fist and thrown away. Many children ran to get it back. The boy who had informed Sehdev and later Jitte's granny yelled at the top of his voice, '*Dadi*, don't go back, I will get it back for you!' Well, he wanted full action that day.

6

Kissu's primary matter of fame in the village school, from class five to ten, was the fact that he had spent five previous years of his schooling in Arunachal Pardesh where his uncle was posted in the army. With a dramatic multitude of stories about that distant land that we saw in the map, he built a formidable reputation by telling spicy anecdotes from the mysterious land. The sluggish and stagnant air in the classroom would instantly vanish as the flurried notes of his hair-raising episodes touched our boyish hearts. Most of these were elephant stories, allegedly based on his own direct experiences with the pachyderms. His well-spun stories had a lot of scope to adjust and get digested in our boyhood imagination. Now but they seem too outlandish.

After matriculation, at the Industrial Training Institute (ITI) at the district town, he accumulated even more reputation. The Bollywood was spinning sylvan and sublime dreams of a hero with his ameliorative touch to undo the hideous deformities plaguing the society, especially the molestation of women, where the hero suddenly jumped among dozens of *goondas* and saved the honor of the damsel in distress, love would blossom then, followed by lots of dance and songs. He carried a hockey stick doing justice to the Bollywood heroes of the eighties and nineties who saved the society, especially the women in distress.

He walked with a perfectly puffed-up chest; his heroism and macho attitude seeking an opportunity to save some damsel in distress. Those were the times when the roadways buses carried a passenger load at least four times more than their full capacity. It was always an ill-omened adventure. You had to push into the throng with devil's impunity. And when you emerged out of the stuffed box you felt misshapen to your last bone.

During one such scuffle among the multitudes to get a foothold onboard, a girl lost her footing at the crowded footboard as the bus started to crawl slowly. The driver usually drove it at a snail's pace for a couple of minutes to allow the throng the last chance on any square centimeter of the bus still available for grabbing. The bus was moving very slowly and this girl softly slumped down. It wasn't a hard fall, she just lost balance. There wasn't a single scratch on her. She would have jumped back to regain her vertical. But that brief moment gave Kissu the opportunity to save his heroine like a Bollywood hero. He hoisted the shaken girl in his worked-out arms and started running. She was perfectly alright and had all the reasons to believe that it was an attempt to kidnap her in broad daylight.

Kissu thought himself to be the savior hero but to her he was nothing short of the most gruesome villain who played with the honor of women. She started beating him with her fists. His face got a lot of blows. Many people ran to rescue her. After getting a few thwacks on his body by other heroes, who came running to rescue the girl, a much perturbed Kissu couldn't make out why he was rewarded that way for his good did.

'I was taking her to the hospital!' he shouted in wonderment, still facing the barrage of many fists.

'Sometimes, even a few seconds delay in reaching the hospital is a matter of life and death!' he hollered his logic over the din.

'Take your mother and your sister to the hospital, you fool!' the girl shrieked with such a look of abhorrence in her eyes that Kissu instantly knew she thought him to be the cruelest *goonda* ever.

ᵖᵖᵖ

Coming from a deprived and underprivileged social strata, that requires one to hone a wide repertoire of survival techniques on a daily basis, Kala is now getting a foothold in the new trade. Befogged by tiny pinpricks in the back alleys, when one emerges on the main thoroughfare, it seems nothing short of a fresh dilemma. But braving against all odds, he has firmly established himself as a dependable vegetable hawker.

Earlier he struggled to remember even the name list of the vegetables loaded in his cart. He sounded plucky and lacking confidence in his shouts. But practice makes a man perfect. 'I have been shouting all these names in the privacy of the fields. But the problem is that I have crammed the entire series. I have to speak all of it. Problem arises when the item that I have shouted isn't found in my cart and then they complain that if I don't have that particular vegetable why did I shout its name. I try to cut out the names of the missing vegetables on a day but then I forget the entire series,' he confided in me.

But he seems to have crammed a long series, longer than anything that he memorized during his few years of schooling. The villagers may keep grumbling but he keeps shouting the names of his vegetables like children shout while playing.

In his mid-forties now, he honorably spent three decades in the testing job of a daily wage laborer. He worked with consummate zeal and carried out tasks with amazing physical felicity. He lifted weights with throwaway ease. His vision's breadth was limited to the tasks required by a mason's helper. He mastered it eloquently. But then he started to feel a bizarre pull at his knees. His knees wobbled and gave arthritic pain. His life was thrown out of gear because he couldn't perform the heavy duty of a mason's helper anymore.

He had to dig deep into the repertory of his faculties to seek an alternative. He turned the spotlight on another source of living. He saw so many *Biharis* wandering the streets as vegetable hawkers and decided to join their league. But his rendition of vegetable names was far below par. They sent down shrill, fluid, distinctive notes of their products, while he gave muffled, dithering notes. In any case, here he is at his best after lots of cramming attempts in the solitude of the agricultural farms.

Pulling a rickshaw laden with vegetables seems a cakewalk to him. 'It's almost no work. I just have to walk around and shout!' he tells gleefully. Little does he realize that salesmanship is a totalized endeavor requiring many traits to fleece, cajole and bind the customers. His sales are lowest among the vegetable hawkers. The people complain that his vegetables aren't fresh. 'Start buying from me first, so that I save some money and buy costlier fresh ones,' he tells them.

Above all, he is happy at least in matching his rivals in yelling out the names of vegetables. Most importantly, he finds the job very easy. Well, everything is relative. His new job is almost no work to him. There are but broken-spirited vegetable sellers who move around as if the entire world's responsibility is on their shoulders. The reason is that they haven't gone through the furnace of plain physical drudgery like Kala has. In order to digest your current standing, take some time off and try some harder job. You will then realize the significance of your undertaking.

ᑭᑭᑭ

Gopu's mother has always believed that he has all that it takes to be a fighter pilot. The reason being that he always stood above his twin brother Lopu in studies. Lopu would come last in the class but Gopu beat his brother and emerge victorious as second last. He always scored two or three more marks than his brother who scored in the vicinity of thirty somethings. More importantly, Gopu would break toy planes in childhood and try to assemble the broken parts. 'He has a fancy for planes!' his mother would gush with pride. I think he had better fancy for breaking and crashing them.

And why was Gopu's mother so sure that he would become a fighter pilot? Apart from getting two marks more than his brother, he made amazing paper planes and would not settle for any other toy than a plane, which he would try to crash in the most innovative ways. Well, that's how mothers are. Their love is always there, irrespective of what we become.

They grew to be big-bottomed, chubby guys with lots of fat around them after completing their senior secondary schooling. Money was somehow arranged to send them to Canada on student visa. 'We aren't going there to study. That's just for visa. We are going to work there!' they declared. And true to their words, they are now making the most of their limited work hours allowed under the student visa. They work as courier delivery guys and have saved a few thousand dollars. The stories of their success have started to do rounds in the housing society where their parents live. The amount is calculated in Indian rupees and that makes them celebrities in the gated society.

On being reminded about the fighter pilot project, their mother says, 'Oh, they are already earning a pilot's salary. It carries risks also in plying fighter planes.'

They won't have inspired so many coming-of-age youngsters in their housing society by becoming fighter pilots as they have done by earning dollars as courier delivery guys in Canada. The parents cite them as examples on the topic of making money and setting a career. A few parents are now taking tips from the successful twins about the ways and means of following their footsteps.

ဖြစ်ဖြစ်

As the stalled education system grappled with the Covid-time shutdown of schools, the institutions tried to provide some succor to the anxious parents by going for online classes. It was something superficial and half-baked but the show had to go on and the little students needed to be reminded daily that there are things called studies, school, class, book and teachers.

Suddenly a new set of instructions flashed on Nevaan's mother's phone. The teachers wanted a plain background during the online classes. The reason was that one student sat by an aquarium during the class. So instead of paying heed to the alphabets, the students had a good online discussion about the fish, which one is a good fish, which one is bad, who is the Papa fish or Mama fish. Taking inspiration from it, the next day a tiny girl sat with her cat. Then someone found his dog in the class initiating parleys about cats and dogs. So now to avoid the extra load of new and newer topics, the overworked online teachers want a plain white background behind all the students.

ᗌᗌᗌ

Some people have such incorruptible, indomitable sense of discipline that they would literally make it a credo of their life to avoid any kind of debasement and deformity to the laboriously polished veneer on their persona. *Tau* Karan Singh had such a disciplined, well ordered and perfectly set-up life off duty that even the duty hours in uniform as an army man stood out a liberal spree of pleasantries and fun. He maintained his well-disciplined tempo, while his peers appeared simply limping and hobbling on the path like errant brats. Any comparison was out of cards.

After retirement, and his routine of thought, action, speech and behavior still more firmly etched in the sacred book of a well-spelt, managed life, he slightly lost the legendary equanimity of mind only in one instance. The stubborn buffalo, ever caught in the ignoble excrescence of indiscipline in its dull brain, tested his patience, the main bulwark of his disciplined life, which stood unruffled even during wars.

Well, there is a pleasanter side to even very grim affairs. Talk to any soldier who has been stationed in Ladhak, he will talk of snows and multi-pronged sorrows in the barren desert. But mention Ladhak to *Tauji* and an august, illustrious and vivifying smile would surface on his gentle features. It was a very soft smile but you could feel its subterranean sprawl, its vastness in his soul. You just could feel it. The ravishing immensity of those memories would take him in its soft embrace. The precipitous slopes and climatic malignity lost their meaning. You could see that his soul was dancing in inexorable joviality with some fond memories. He would smile and have a lungful of tented kitchen warmth and aroma. 'Well, the butter toast, fruit jam and tea in the snows tasted far better than anything I have ever eaten in my life!' he would recall the taste in his mouth, as if lost in a dream, his soul sorteying on sublime promenades in those high barren mountains.

Coming back to the buffalo, she would go into the farthest recesses of the village pond, forcing the ex-soldier to wade his way across the bunch-grass and pinching shrubbery lest she escaped into the countryside for an undisciplined furlough. Both of them would return after a few hours. Her horns adorned with muddy clumps of grasses, promiscuous signs of her indiscipline and revelry.

Tauji, who would have thought hundred times before reprimanding even a Chinese or Paki soldier if they crossed the border inadvertently, finally lost his patience and would chastise the disorderly beast. '*Sali!*' he would mutter as he gave it a tiny rap on its haunches. This exclamation turned into a regular affair, given the buffalo's freewheeling indiscipline, so much so that the villagers started to address the buffalo as his son's *Mausiji*.

ᖰᖰᖰ

The honeycomb in the curry-leaf tree is a buxom round thing now. It serves to have some flowers in your garden. It gives an opportunity to the honeybees to survive for some more time in your area. I keep my eyes ready for the lone honey buzzard that sometimes scans the skies for some odd honeycomb somewhere. Apart from some innocent plunders during childhood, I have never tried to take away honey from a comb. It is as bad as someone taking money from my account. Its smell and sight are my primary takeaways. Maybe they sense and feel safe this way because the honeybees stay almost permanently in the yard.

The sky ponders with an infinitely impersonal look. There are hundreds of marigolds basking under the hazy sunrays of December. In the afternoon, a pale sun shining upon the unassuming flowers, I find the bees almost dozing in calm slumber after getting overfed on the pollen. Look at these little things and an instinct's illumination, shrouded in the ordinary promptings of a common man, turns it a beautiful world.

The cats are growing finely and the coquettish mysteries cajoling from outside the fence turn them more out-bound these days. Desire is in incubation and they seem to have a liking for cat girls. It means the dove's eggs are safe so far. At least the eggs may hatch. Beyond that I don't see much of a chance. It's such a careless, flimsy nest of sinewy twigs, so low and almost public, that some eagle will have a bigger hatchling breakfast in lieu of the cats missing on the egg breakfast.

In the next-door granduncle's house, all Labrador Tuffy can do is to bark at the monkeys. He cannot scale walls and jump over roofs like them. One or the other monkey purposefully sits at a point visible to the helpless dog. The clever monkeys keep changing their post, and the sentry Labrador goes barking through the day. He has to realize that one shouldn't test one's lungs over the issues about which one cannot do much.

ᗡᗡᗡ

Espousing a keen sense to follow the conventionalities, and somehow handle the hormonal-led heightened palpitations of early youth desire, Ballu got married at sixteen, became father at seventeen, a grandfather at thirty-five when his eldest daughter gave birth to a girl. Imbued with the routine colors of a mundane low-income household, any little pleasure comingled with lots of pain as if in payment to the former, harrowed by continuously evolving challenges, trying to forget the painful constriction of life through cheap liquor, in the next ten years he had many grandchildren.

Sadly, his youngest grandson was born with congenital defect concerning food canal and the respiratory system. A complicated surgery followed. The infant didn't survive but he left his mark—a bill of three and half lakh rupees to be settled by the poor family. They are landless daily wage earners. It meant they had to borrow the money. Now life and living will exact a bit higher price from them. But they aren't crestfallen. 'After all, we come to this world to do exactly these kinds of things only,' he philosophizes.

ဇဇဇ

The village schools of the eighties of the last century were the places where the domineering teachers ruled with illimitable authority and iron hand. Physically strong teachers trampled down any impertinent sign in the class with an alarming tenacity. They had a predilection for using their arms more than their brains. The students from the peasantry class were full of mischief and one needed a lot of iron-will to keep them subdued so as to at least retain them within the premises. Education and Jat farmers was a definite misalliance.

In good moods, they would have weighty puns as well. But the saturine shadow of their fickle moods always lingered on the premises. The teachers who created the maximum fear among the students were, by default, the best teachers among the peasantry. To crown it all, the best teachers were those who broke maximum number of sticks.

There were but some docile teachers, either on account of their mild temperament or lack of physical proportions to turn into a bull on rampage. These docile teachers suffered maybe even more than the students. The students would be kicked, tossed about, yelled at, thwacked and tomahawked by the bullying, big teachers. The beaten pupils would then target the docile teachers. Master Aggarwal was pretty harmless in this regard. Short, chubby, bald, with cute jowls, like Mr. Pickwick, he offered the chink in the stony teacher rampart. No wonder, the students targeted him. The students would pour out their entire vengeance against the teachers as a 'class'. In a chilling conflagration of mischief, he was given the funniest names possible on earth. More rowdy type of students even misbehaved with him outrightly.

He was born and brought up in the nearest town and commuted daily to face the ordeal. It was like setting out a caged bird into a deep forest suddenly. He didn't know the *desi* words in the farming slang. The students took advantage of it. If a student went missing for the day, he would inform him that their *bitoda* had fever. And Master Aggarwal would agree to it, thinking someone at home fell sick. Little did he know that *bitoda* stood for the conical structure for storing dung-cakes.

But then he kept his fight on. He kept a short stick and if striking wasn't his forte, he would prod in the ribs and try to draw some painful cry from the inveterate souls. He also tried to fight on the nomenclature front. He called students '*abe kambal*', '*abe khesh*', '*abe chaddar*', '*abe pyjama*' based on the most ubiquitous item upon the student's person.

Kaptan troubled him a lot. Master Aggarwal taught us Mathematics. It was our quarterly test and he arrived with the bundle of evaluated answer sheets. The students but won't wait for him to start distributing the answer sheets and harangued him a lot. Kaptan as usual was pretty vocal in this. One of the last students in class, as far as marks were concerned but probably first in playing truant, he was very confident this time. During the examination, he was sitting after me and copied with an unbelievable attention. He wrote for the entire three hours. 'I have never written this much in my entire life,' he told me after the exam.

Master Aggarwal gave the sum and summary of the results before he started handing over the sheets to the students: 'Sandeep scores hundred and Kaptan gets zero.'

Kaptan hardly knew anything about mathematics so almost the entire scribbling hadn't any meaning. He couldn't believe that so many written pages failed to get him even a single mark. But then he had his own interpretation. Master Aggarwal had very proudly written Zero in flowing alphabets. The Z looked like number three and the over-zealous 'ero' looked like three zeroes. That gave Kaptan the right to claim that he had actually scored 3000 out of 100.

$$ಐಐಐ$$

Colors represent the mirthful gratuity of mother nature. The void, the nothingness gets striped with sacramental plentitude of membranous manifestations of an entire array of colors. All it takes is just a few colors to transmute the dull, plastid screen into a lively drama.

Colors speak a lot about our personality as well. The colors of cars, for example. Whenever I see a red car on the road, I brace myself for some extra caution. The red cars seem to whizz past with infernal temper. They look highly competitive and seem eager to smite away any other vehicle in speed and attitude. They gesticulate quite forcefully and look like a big siren warning you to stay away. The people driving red cars carry a bit of extra adrenaline, which is helpful for fun and adventure but is pushy for those around. Moreover, extra adrenaline on the road is an inappropriate setting. So give them enough space as they go raising a tornado on the road.

As I went lazily on my scooter on the road, going to the nearest town, mulling over the credits and debits of life, the red signal flashed in the rear-view mirror. Instantly I left the entire road to the red-gallant. You are blameworthy if you don't do it, especially in case of angry red bigger vehicles than yours. Do it to avoid any gruesome spectacle. As it passed arbitrarily shoving away any opposition, flaunting its extraordinary stature, the windy storm was enough to shake me and my tiny two-wheeled machine. My stewardship pretty heavily shaken, I went still slower.

After fifteen minutes, I reached a congested crossing in the town. On a packed road in towns, the two wheelers carry some advantage. They need little space so that you can maneuver among the bigger vehicles stranded for space. As I slowly trudged ahead, I saw the red car. I crossed it with a self-styled smirk. The tortoises still win the races, after all. The Indian roads are a great leveler. To allay the fears of slow movers, let me point out that the costliest cars cannot fly. And the pony carts and slow guys like me have as much chance in reaching the destination as any of the costliest, reddest car.

Then there was a sight to behold my attention in the town. A golden retriever proves that it's indeed a capable retriever. At the confectionary shop, it knows which biscuits to retrieve to match the spools of pleasantry in its mood. With an admixture of loyalty and authority, it walks by the side of its master, safely holding the biscuit packet in its mouth.

ppp

A basket is toppled. With typical simian assiduity, a mama monkey meddles with peace in the courtyard. The tiny imp on her back holds a raw banana as she expertly escapes. I can just bang a hollow bamboo on the parapet wall. She beautifully glides in air as she jumps to the other roof across the twelve-foot wide street. The baby safely perched on her back and holding the green banana as the trophy of their effort gives me a taunting, smirking look, as if to say, 'You are no match for my mama!'

Even the doves, despite the foreordained tragedy about to take place in the scraggy, sparse nest, sometimes go against their nature and turn a fighter. A docile dove is a beautiful sight but to have these lovely cooing moments they need to fight with talons sometimes. It enkindles some faint hope for the hatchling in the nest—it's a miracle that at least one egg was spared and there is a funny, hairless plump chick, forcing me to count it as a success even if it dies the same day. But there is every chance that you will be disappointed if you nurture hopes about the doves successfully raising a brood. I haven't seen a single successful case in dozens of episodes witnessed over the decades.

The conspicuous calls of the long-tailed rufous treepie carry reminiscences from the hills. Sometimes they seem throwing a weighty pun at the local birds. It's a migrant couple with cinnamon body, black head and bluish grey long graduated tail. These treepies are known to keep a covetous eye for the eggs and hatchlings of smaller birds. So the little ball of meat in the dove's fragile, clearly visible nest has caught the treepie's attention. The predator makes frequent forays to taste it. The doves don't stand a chance against an eagle. But they think they can give it a fight against the treeepie. The moment the treepie lands on the curry-leaf tree, the doves turn soldierly and chase it away. The intruder takes off with a loud and shrill *ko-ko-ko-ko*. It kept coming for three days but the doves defended well.

As I have emphasized it many times, a dove hatchling needs to be very lucky to survive. The resident cats have smelt feline girls outside the fence. It meant at least the eggs survived. It seems the honey buzzer has found honey somewhere else, so it hasn't turned up for the last few days. And now the challenger to its survival happens to be a treepie against which the docile doves can feign bravery for some time. Accepted that we need luck to survive but effort is luck's operational part.

פּפּפּ

Here is beautiful story of love, faith, prayers and persistence. A nasty tornado strikes Kentucky. It's a countryside house. A grandma with her fifteen-month-old granddaughter and three-month old grandson is all there to protect the two little angels. You don't have the physical force to fight a tornado but you have a still more potent power in you to do it, prayers.

The storm's eye lurks viciously. The old lady knows the house is just moments away from being blown off. She puts the kids in a bathtub and swathes them in pillows and blankets. More importantly, she puts a Bible with them and says prayers over them.

The tornado strikes the house. The house is blown off. The bathtub is picked off the floor and is blown away. The rescue workers find it at a distance, upturned among the telltale signs of the storm's mauling. They lift it and hand over the kids to their granny. They are safe. Prayers indeed can help us in braving the strongest tornados of life.

ᐁᐁᐁ

One year of preparatory schooling put enough burden on three-year-old Nevaan. The classrooms look almost like poor ghettos to mere two-year olds made to sit, already under the disciplinarian stick. Then the pandemic-facilitated lockdown was a big respite for these tiny students. KG 1 and KG 2 went through online mode without claiming too much from the rich bounty of childhood. The online classes were a big fun initially. Not going to the school is a big bonus to any child. It's really joyful. But then the idea of joy is already relative. Now the one-hour online class has started to sound tedious. And off day from this session comes as joy presently. So the other day when he was expecting a full holiday, the message popped up that there will be a thirty-minute fun activity class today. 'Oh no, even today we have school!' he gets irritated.

ᐁᐁᐁ

The scientists are taking up their domains with a legendary integrity. Every inch on earth is under our sweeping ambit. So we are chronicling space odysseys. The terrestrial miracles have been regularized to an extent to turn them most mundane things possible. The earth is littered with our rampant desires' jargon. There is a dangerous fallacy at work but it comes attired as the new-age holism. So we are now space bound like Vasco de Gama and Columbus explored hitherto unseen lands.

The low-earth orbit has three thousand satellites. And thousands more are in the pipeline. Among this overcrowding, the risks of collisions are emerging at a grave rate. Then we will have a very lucrative profession of space-cleaners. The trash collector, who just asked me if I have any stack of old newspapers to sell, has to know that his sons and grandchildren will have the chance to clean space if they will persist in the trade and use the latest technology, like the rest of the traditional occupations are adopting new technologies.

The grain merchants in Delhi have their grandsons working on laptops to manage what was earlier done in fat red-cloth bound account books. In Chawdi Bazaar in Delhi, in a tiny few square yard space crammed with nuts, bolts and the portly grandfather, hardly leaving any space in the tiny cubicle of a shop, the educated grandson is tucked in a corner and trying online selling. So maybe the coming generations of these trash pickers will turn tech savvy and take their endeavors to collect trash in the space.

ᗾᗾᗾ

In order to survive, a dove's hatchling needs the best of luck from all angles possible. It seems a fickle, vacillating and indecisive parenting. They need their guardian angels to be at maximum alert to thwart the renegadely lurking agents of death. The nest is so fragile and small, almost hitting high notes of imperishment as the bizarre, complicated sub-plots of life and death unfold around. It's an almost see-through, flat assemblage of thin twigs placed at almost a public place, among easily reachable branches at a hand's reach. Its mere sight giving a pickling and grilling push to the taste buds of many a predatory bird. The souls of cats getting into stir-frying and deep-frying mode at the culinary prospects.

You need to make a substantive leap of faith to collect any rhyme or reason on the question of how do they even survive as a species. The nest bears such a frustrating anatomy that even by a gentle breeze the egg or the hatchling may plop down by itself to the delight of brooding dark shadows of mortality. So among the boiling and steaming culinary scenarios, if a creamy-white egg survives and a hatchling comes out, even this can be taken as a successful nesting. As the burgeoning, cascading clamor of life moves on, the majority of the hatchlings survive for a few days at the most. It's a miracle that the doves still survive as a species. It seems impossible without prompt, belligerent defense by mother existence itself. Maybe mother nature sets up a miraculous scheme of chance factors to keep some odd baby bird alive.

The cats are in love, following freaky mirages most of the time, so their absence in the garden means that one egg out of three survived. The other two were taken by the guest treepie after the expletive-rich fight that went for three days, rewarding it with two eggs. The rufous brown and pale chestnut bird kept threatening and blustering for three days to chuck out two out of three eggs.

The honey buzzard seems to be away on its poaching foray. It hasn't been seen for a few weeks even though there is a bigger honeycomb near the dove hatchling.

The treepie then returned with a whippy and aggressive attitude to have a heavy lunch on the hatchling also. The doves, with their tentative gazelle looks, fought tooth and nail to foil its efforts. But a crow, spurred by a thieving itch, unapologetically swooped down to clutch the prize with an eerie precision to give the little one its first and the last flight. Now, the laughing dove is crying through its chuckling notes. To the uninformed audience she must be sounding laughing. But I know her situation and feel her pain oozing through her ripply, cuddling laughing chuckles.

Isn't it that most of our instinctive reactions and the consequent emotions of anger, hate, jealousy, fear and prejudices are born of our ignorance of the reality surrounding that individual? It's so easy to get judgmental of someone without being aware of the complete picture. Like taking the cries of a distraught dove as joyful chuckles! So it helps to know a bit more about people and their situations beyond a point that merely appears on the surface.

7

Little Nevaan is at a temple with his *Mausiji*. With innocently garlanding ease, a kid has crammed many Sanskrit *slokas*, so no wonder he is the centre of attraction. With an acrobat's agile leap, he jumps from slogan to slogan, garnering heaps of praise from those around. Poor Nevaan is already tired with practicing alphabets and numbers on the slate board and assembling and reading educational puzzles before coming to the temple. And now this irrational and idiosyncratic chanting by this chit of a boy. As if there is a savory slice of lime pickle in his mouth, which he likes with an impeccable and uncomplicated sense of cherishment, Nevaan tries to divert the show in his direction.

With the urgency of rattling trams and angrily hawking vendors, he recites *Gayatri Mantra* and *Mahamritunjya Mantra*. Egged on by the heady pampering of his parents, the other child unleashes *sloka* after *sloka* from his big repertoire. Coming to terms with a sense of humane realism, little Nevaan brings out the best shot in his kitty. He starts whistling. It's his inalienable right to showcase what he considers to be the best item in his kitty. He hammers his tone to stonewall the Sanskrit *slokas* coming out so profusely.

Only a gentleman with silver-grey hair tries to be the solo audience to his offering. Nevaan fails to grab attention. So the other boy wins the show—prominently, purposefully and publicly. On top of it, it gets him another reprimand from his ever-correcting mama. He responds. At night, his mama opens her phone to find a notification from her Amazon account regarding a payment failure of one lakh rupees. Nevaan put an i-phone and a gold ring in the cart and made an unsuccessful attempt at payment. He knows his mom loves the money more in the purse instead of its changing forms, especially the costly gadgets.

There is a visitor at the house. He is haggling him with the question, 'When did you come *beta*?' Now little Nevaan is clueless about dates and days. It was about two weeks ago when he arrived at his maternal uncle's house, yours truly by the way. The questioner looks serious enough to have his answer at any cost. He repeats the question a few times. 'I came on the day I came here,' Nevaan gives the asker a crisp glimpse of his much-sought answer.

I'm reading and little Nevaan is looking for something more substantial, a playmate. Lost in the reclusive and remote world contained in the book, I try to ignore him. He is making strange guttural sounds. 'What is this?' I'm forced to enquire. 'I'm asking "What are you doing?" in Chinese,' he enlightens me. 'I'm reading a book,' I reply in Hindi to his Mandarin query. 'No, no I'm asking what are you doing in reading,' he simplifies the query. I make it that maybe he wants to know what I'm reading. 'I'm reading that little kids shouldn't disturb the elders when they are reading a book,' I try to somehow salvage my reading session. This piece of information doesn't fit his plan at all. 'No, no I was just asking what are you doing,' he tries to avoid the unbecoming issue of kids disturbing book-reading elders.

And before I can reply he says, 'Ok, I see you are playing with a book.' He continues with his strange sounds. The answer to his second main question doesn't exist because the question itself has been wiped clean on his slate.

By the way, his mother is very happy. 'He has started to get up in *Inglish* now!' she gushes. 'Today he said, "I'm *oothing* in the morning," and last night he said, "I'm sleeping," so that means he is sleeping in *eengleesh* also!' Well, this world seems to be some primeval mother's creation.

I'm engrossed in the miseries of the bigger world. The paper spread in front of my face carries deep and voluminous folds of activities that grown-ups are engaged in. Geostrategic wars, political brawls, diseases, killings, sports rivalries holding my attention with their clawy tentacles. I'm sitting on a chair. Little Nevaan is standing in front of me. He is a bundle of energy carrying ecumenical vibrancy and a dreamy future-map in his twinkling eyes. I'm, on the other hand, carrying a timeworn load born of weathering of long years. No wonder, our worlds are completely different.

The double spread newspaper chronicles a sage of grit and glories of the past twenty-four hours. He is staring at the full-page luscious advertisement by a global food chain. Crunchy grilled patty, juicy toasted buns and grilled burgers are presented for a child's food paradise. A picture speaks thousands of words. He has read entire tomes by the time I finish reading a few news columns. 'Sufi mama, why aren't you reading? You are just looking at the a, b, c, d. Read here. Yummy yummy *masala mar ke*, aha!' he informs me that he has read all the pictures and I have been merely looking at the letters in the meantime.

He has turned a big informer in the house now. The gossiping neighborhood aunties use his informing skills. 'Don't tell what you hear inside the house to the people outside!' he gets a reprimand from his mother. So he decides not to inform anyone about anything said inside the house anymore. 'Ma doesn't call you bulldozer auntie. Ma doesn't say that your car is *khatara* uncle ji. Ma never says that you beat uncle with a stick aunty ji,' he tries his best not to divulge any secret anymore. He is very happy as he returns. 'Ma, I didn't tell them anything as you said,' he tells her and expects ice cream as a reward today.

He is around three and is taken to the doctor for a routine vaccine. He howls. All his wrongs for which he gets reprimanded flash before his terrified eyes. He thinks he is getting a punishment for all those pieces of mischief. 'Dotter, dotter, please forgive me! *Maaf kar do*! I will stop eating candies. I will not watch mobile. I will stop watching cartoons on TV. I will study,' he realizes all the sins that have possibly landed him in trouble. After a long list of will-nots, he realizes his sins are too big for these promises. Then he tries to bribe, 'Dotter, I will give you the best plane, the red fighter plane!' The doctor is amused. 'O really! I will take it as my fees.' The needle goes in. A loud cry. The tone is bordered on the abusive frequency. His mother senses it. She tries to forestall it by putting her hand on his mouth but Nevaan is successful in splurging a cuss word he has caught in the streets from the mouths of older street urchins.

We buy a new cycle with side-supporters on so that he learns the art of paddling and balancing. He is serious and sullen and sits in a corner. 'Aren't you happy with this beautiful gift?' we ask. 'No, I'm not happy. Now I have to fall from it many times!' he explains the reason for his being in sullen mood. He has seen a few little ones toppling over as they learnt cycling. 'What gift is this? I have to fall many times to play with it. No, no it's not a good one,' he condemns the latest purchase.

He is getting another dose of reprimand. He has written 'Pupaya' on his worksheet. The last papaya he ate didn't come too sweet. So he improvised to make it sweeter. 'But Ma, pupaya is very sweet,' he tries to convince her. Maybe pupaya is sweeter than papaya. But in the world of grown-ups, the helplessness to adhere to the factual correctness doesn't leave any space for the sweetness brought by a kid by changing some vowel.

The other day, after two hours of memorizing and writing exercise, he writes 'Grabs' for 'Grapes.' His mother gets a practical clue and grabs him by head and shakes it quite forcefully to ruffle his nicely done hair. He looks shaken like a pigeon cat-handled by an angry cat. He doesn't react, he responds. 'Ma, you tell what is two plus, minus, multiply a, b, c, d, dog and cat!' he yells his question.

ᢡᢡᢡ

The spirit of commerce is zealously relishing its sway over the modern-day mass psyche. All our passions, prejudices, pride and myriad other silent inconsistencies of our character go onto feed the spirit of the corporate operating with an officious smile, promising enduring homilies and affinities. Even the artless, hardworking rural rustic society is falling into the sheen of the corporate. There are entrepreneurs wandering in the streets, like this hawker who is shouting, 'Get eyesight glasses. Get your eyes checked and get a *number ka chasma* so that you can see even an ant on your neighbor's wall.'

Well-qualified ophthalmologists beware now. He is a small thin man with a testing kit on his bicycle. These are the times of doorstep delivery of products and services. Even the malls look like a kind of obligation now. There are so many people who are open to the idea of delivering anything from needles to road engines to your doorstep. Every street has a peasant woman selling garments and clothes apart from buttermilk and milk. One provides dung-cakes also. I recall a very kind-hearted, ever-smiling, loving custom clearing agent. Mention procuring a fighter jet to him. '*Ho jayega*, worry not!' he is always there to help you keep your hopes alive.

ᐅᐅᐅ

A few weeks back, 65-year-old Randhir, a hardworking farmer, happily shared the exploits of his two-year-old grandson. The kid is surely large for his years. 'He shakes up and bashes all the children including four-year-olds,' he shares the proud, panoramic characterization of the upholder of his pedigree. 'He is strong, I can see,' the grandfather is already mulling over his future as a famous wrestler.

The kid must have felt the encouraging vibes emanating from his grandfather. But the proud grandpa should know that kids basically hone their skills—good, bad and all—within the house to begin with. So even the grizzly bear look of the grandmother, a strong peasant woman, was not sufficient to deter the little wrestler from making her the object of his fun exploits. Carrying his exploits a nice notch higher, he hit her with an iron blowpipe on her knee. It was a painful strike leaving her in an ennui and indecision whether to throttle the perpetrator or to heave him over her head and then dump as a punishment. But a crisp articulation of the intent to defend her child by the boy's mother, herself a big woman so much so that when she decked herself for town visits she looked like a caparisoned jumbo, deterred the ageing matriarch from carrying out her intent. She went limping for many days.

'The boy did what I always intended to do but could never do it for the plain fear of her,' Randhir secretively mused. There have been long and sluggish decades of their matrimonial innings, both of them trying the art of scapegoating to find fault with each other in their routine farming life full of challenges at many fronts. You could sense the oppositional molecules floating in the air whenever they were together. The plain fact is that the sturdy woman, all along these years, has been strong enough to pin him down in a hand-to-hand combat and emerge winner with a clear verdict. So he is happy that his little grandson has done what he failed to do in decades.

Little did he realize that the children love to have fresher objects to carry out their commendable feats. Randhir is far away in the serene precincts of a peaceful place in sleep. Suddenly he is jolted out of his siesta by a painful strike on his head. The kid gallant is seen grinning holding the peasant's favorite *danda*. He saw stars in the day forming constellations holding staggering forecasts for the lamp of their pedigree. But he somehow checked his impulse to beat the boy like a young errant colt. He closed his eyes and tried to regain his dream world.

Another strike and this time he swipes to clutch the culprit but the attacker slips away. Randhir now knows the offender has to be taught a lesson. He feigns to sleep. The fun-loving boy stealthily creeps up to him and before he aims his third strike, Randhir comes to life like an old, black panther. The little antelope is in his grasp. He picks up his *chappal* and gives four cool strikes at the little marauder's bum. The boy now maintains distance and doesn't stealthily approach his grandfather when he sleeps. He thinks his grandpa feigns sleep especially to lure him to strike and then grab him to beat him.

᠉᠉᠉

It's a balmy afternoon on December 31, 2021. The sun-warmed moments are sleepwalking their way to a cold evening. The last hours of the year on the peripheral, marginal sprawl of another time unit readying to say goodbye. Time and its slipperiness, it elusive prowl reaping sheaves of lives with the scythe in its hand. Space and time in an emblematic tussle, laying out a well-manicured matrix of things, phenomena and happenings.

There are the thinnest sparse traces of white in the blue skies, some kind of little commas in the seamless narrative of mother existence. It turns the afternoon blaze to a kind of yellowish tinge. The sky looking down with an unpretentious grace as the earthlings' vaulting desires hurtle up to form a cosmos of their own.

The frost-beaten trees hang there with their attitude of tortuous durability. The sparrows are engaged in sharing chatty tips. A tiny group of six or seven parrots goes with their thrilling and fascinating squawking as if discussing the seamless fabric of fruity flavors. A flock of pigeons, a few dozen of them—maybe around hundred—flies in a beautiful formation as if drawn by the smell of some unusual delights. Every time they turn southwards, their white underwings flash a silvery blaze in perfect symmetry. What a celebration of the spirit of freedom! We humans may harbor traces of melancholy but they are bidding a happy goodbye to 2021. And their formation and the flashing of the silvery underwings against the sunrays, as they dive in a particular direction, exposing the whitish underparts of their wings to the sunrays, beats any aerial show managed by we humans to commemorate our victories, national days or other landmarks in our history. It's a subtle, simplistic saga and augurs well for the coming year. We have to hope for the better because mother nature is splashing her joy with such prominence through the emblematic agents of peace.

ԲԲԲ

As the ever-effacing scythe of time reaps on, it's no longer the same world. We have turned out to be a sensationalist species. Our riling and abrasive march on the path has forced the lesser species to go hush-hush and move prohibitively, trying to stay away from our snipes and barbaric barbs.

But our simian friends, the co-sharers of our gloriously compulsive traits, still hold out the baton from the side of the lower species. Everything from flowers to jewellery is under risk. How can things be normal with so many monkeys around? The situation is grim. Sometime in future, I apprehend a 'Planet of the Apes' kind of scenario.

The rhesus monkeys aren't simply driven by instincts. They surely have a strong intent to carry out their thuggery. They love breaking, ruffling, toppling and shuffling things. To watch their misdeeds is an illustrated treat in itself. They deftly handle the myriad strands of foolhardiness to spin out most outrageous of stage scenes. Their sexuality is decidedly warped like their more evolved brethren. I see two monkeys going normally over the top of a wall. Suddenly, the one behind jumps onto the haunches of the one in front and feigns vigorous, avaricious pelvic thrusts to pacify the pangs of lust lying forever unsatisfied in the psychic realms. It's a blatant slap on our norms. A typical tome of their mischief.

ᐅᐅᐅ

This particular *belpatra* tree, in a corner in our garden, has unbelievably big, dangerous thorns, almost two inches long and so sturdy that these can be safely used as nails plonked into wooden planks. Even standing near the tree seems so scary. Its thorny mass is sprawled over the fence wall. It's impossible to even think for the humans to put their hands through a few boughs. It's a fearsomely barbed fence. But cats, monkeys, squirrels, chameleons scamper through it without much concern. The birds land upon it with as much ease as they show while landing on a flower.

I see two peacocks rustle through the thorny maze almost effortlessly. Their entire bodies seem to carry natural intelligence, allowing them to go along the path of existence with amazing fluidity. We, on the other hand, have too big conscious part in our brains, which clouds our natural intelligence with fears, phobias, illusions and false assumptions. No wonder, I get a prick as and when I try to pluck a leaf from the tree. They, the rest of the non-human species, don't bother beyond a few basic points and glide joyfully in the process of living. We humans, on the other hand, carry a huge burden of awareness that usually brings us down instead of elevating us higher.

ᐅᐅᐅ

Naveen Baman usually set out on his hunt for the day after touching his mother's feet. It was theoretically a very moral-heavy schedule. Much to matrilineal delight, his father would get a patriarchal heartburn as the son won't even look in his direction as he stepped out for a well-paid day in many senses of the term, that included apart from money—his first love—winning some affection from some fresh female in his life.

With each minute ascending into relevance, the mother would wait for her darling son to return at night to serve him dinner, however late it was. She was always there, awake and alert, like a petite watchman on duty. The blooming mechanisms of a very interesting outdoor life got him curious about liquor one day. He tasted it, found it interesting, drank then, and led by an over-zealous assertion of free spirits gulped down pegs after pegs. From the top of an oozing enthusiasm, he toppled down suddenly and was blacked out.

The moment you pass out you turn small and insignificant. With monumental presence of mind, his drinking peers left him in front of his street and vanished into the profoundly dark swathes of night. They were well aware of the fulfilling bond between the mother and the son and hence were scared of the mother's stormy tantrums when she would see her son heaped out of senses.

Clueless about how to proceed further, he chose half of the water drain and the other half of the street to lie down and snore. The air was laden with disintegrating gloominess. Much scandalized over her son's thunderous misjudgment, the mother arrived at the scene with a few members of the extended family to salvage her son from the clutches of the corrupt and corroded episode.

They got into the act of hauling him up. Naveen had very serious objection to this disturbance. The mother was shouting amidst a flurry of teary promos. With his few traces of consciousness still in his grasp, he made out that this old, shrieking woman was the ringleader in dislodging him from his favorite drain. 'Bhola, give me a rope. We have to strangulate this old woman. She has too big a tongue and prattles too much,' he yelled to his cousin brother. The mother indeed was famous for her talkative tongue.

As they dragged him to the house, he kept on shouting, 'We have to kill this woman by hanging!' The father looked from a distance. He felt as if his son was talking sense now, even though under the influence of liquor. But truth has to be accepted in whatever form it arrives. So he felt happy inside.

Naveen started snoring after a tornado of proclamations to get his mother hanged by the strongest rope in the house. The next day, when he got down to touch her feet she kicked him. She did it for a week. On the eighth day, she put her hand on his head. 'You are a nice son! Devils are the ones who made you drink,' she declared.

ᗡᗡᗡ

There are people who once lit up your life with their warm smiles. The cold, hard icicles of your life melted under their warm touch like balmy sunrays giving a kiss of life after many snowy days. Later, however far you may drift apart, they are still inseparable part of your being. Your ego may deny it on the surface but the cells in your body carry those sweet memories. They set up the tunes of an unwavering harmony below the turbulent surface having ripples of guilt, complaint, pain and anger. The fragrance lingers on with its innate modesty. A frozen current inside you that still flows sometimes under the warmth of the nostalgic strains of distant memories. Its aching beauty, its divine sadness still sometimes comes acalling to refresh and revitalize your pain-lynched present self. It always exists to define your present. Always. Acknowledging the existence of countless such sweet memories in my mind, body and spirit! With grace, humility, gratitude and love wishing the source of these sweet memories a very happy birthday! Always wishing that special someone a profound, meaningful, joyful happy birthday on the tenth of January!

ᛈᛈᛈ

The rains of January are not so gentle reminders by mother nature that She holds far more cords in the puppet show of our existence; that all our strategizing is unreliable and dodgy. Sometimes She flaunts her robust patronage of our fates through the harshest, cruelest and darkest trajectory. The January rains may not exactly qualify to be too much on the scale of the fact mentioned above but it has enough to convey her disapproving glare.

The clouds thunder at their best with a strange creative focus, a kind of stimulating contradiction in the form of water and sizzling lightning fire across its watery bowels. It looks a strange, awesome testing ground of hatching newer possibilities.

The cold rain comes lashing. We realize our limitations and withdraw. And a few days of leave of absence by the sun makes us realize that our life is a mere gift by the sun. A brief spell of sunlight amid the entire gloomy overcast day has the power and potential to revive hopes at many levels. The loud, garish proclamations instantly take a backseat as the tiniest of a ray peeps through the clouds. Delicately flavored is its touch; everything looks energetic and inspired. And despite holding the key to our survival, the celestial torchbearer stays so unassuming and unpretentious.

The good part about January rain is that it gives a nice wash to the trees and plants. It serves a still better role. The arrogant monkeys surrender to their wet, soaked fate. The eccentric display of misdemeanors vanishes and they start behaving well. The sight of a shivering, rain-sodden monkey on a gloomy, cold January day, moving with good manners is nothing short of blissful. Their foolhardiness slowly being asphyxiated, they carry a sullen visage. They don't loaf around. No wonder, it's really peaceful when they sit quiet.

Three days of winter rain and their roof leaks. It never was a home, always remained a house. The father-son drunkard pair always kicked the homely foundations. Disgrace, poverty and continuous pain define their existence. And now when the roof leaks in this cold weather, the daughters of the almost ruined house get onto the roof, try to stop the leakages by putting a tarpaulin sheet as an extra protection to their depilated house. The broken house still stands because there are three lovely daughters to support its crumbling columns.

And the winter slowly lumbers on as if following a self-reflecting trail. It's very cold. The reptiles and rodents gone very deep for hibernation in their holes and burrows. Deprived of hunting opportunities, all the feral cats have smartly ditched their shyness and come begging. They raise their tails, making purring, flattering sounds and try to rub against one's legs. It's a problem of plenty. You don't feel comfortable with all the feral cats gone friendly.

Some ray of hope in the winters. The Taliban have made a slight amendment in their behavior. I take it as a welcome change. They have ordered the shop owners to behead mannequins. Well, that's better than beheading people in real life. One little step ahead indeed. But then they follow it with a big jump backwards. They are going to have a suicide squad as a regular unit in their army. This is scary. Someone blowing himself or herself seems the worst form of violence.

SANDEEP DAHIYA

ᐅᐅᐅ

It's a tale of an industrious spiny-leaved sow thistle. It may not be a scenic introduction to a garden but it piques the senses with its meticulous as well as untidy presentation. Though a herb in the scheme of nature, it's condemned as a weed by we humans caught in a morass of radicalism fuelled by our utilitarian spirit. While the little plant stands silently engrossed, swathed in incredulous silence, its tiny flowers carry amazing lightness in smile.

The fragile furor unfolds around. Bouquets and brickbats are flaunted on the basis of what is useful and what is not. The farmers have a particular aversion to its presence in the cropped fields. An entire range of poison has been contrived to kill it. The weedicides are highly effective. You see the revealing, spectacular remains, with our triumph incredibly detailed over the withering nuisance.

The entire farming community baying for its blood, this particular sow thistle looked for a safe corner beyond the farmers' sickle and fumigation showers. It grows there in the circular skylight at the top end of the barn's wall. Old houses with cracks are now perhaps the last refuge of the untamed and the wild strains of nature. The winter rains lashed with a delectable flavor as the sow thistle picked out the tiny crack where the mankind isn't still at war with space, a little crack in the small skylight.

Earlier the monsoon rains lashed. It was well sheltered and a furious rainstorm would give it just a decent amount of water. It thrived with a well-conceived and well-preserved spirit of youth. Then the winter sneaked in with its icy power-trappings. Facing south, it simply soaked tumblers of sunlight in the afternoons as the kind sun streamed from the southern side.

The entire circular skylight is now covered with its luxuriant growth. Its bluish green spiny leaves carry the aura of thinly veiled fiction, a kind of delicate balance between facts and fables. As a mark of its triumph, now it flaunts little yellow flowers that look similar to wild dandelion. There are many flat-topped arrays of flower heads that hold the prospects of a dandelion-type smile on an old, withering wall. There is still hope—a wild plant having a foothold among we humans and smiling breezily. Well, some more flowers are always good for this world.

ᕹᕹᕹ

Nevaan is reading a poem to his father from a WhatsApp message on the latter's phone. His father is correcting every word the little son pronounces. Nevaan's patience is pilfered away and he shuts him up, 'How will I finish the poem Papa? You keep quiet and only say, "*vaah, vaah*!" when I read the poem!'

'Oh, it's Thursday tomorrow!' little Nevaan is suddenly startled. Well, it's the 'thought of the day' day during their online classes. And he *thinks* not so appropriately sometimes. His thoughts sometimes border on big insults for the teachers and the school. His free-spirited thoughts give him ruffled hair and angry shakings by his much-worried mother. 'How I wish there was no Thursday and just Sunday in its place! There should be two Sundays!' he sighs very sadly.

One day he is feeling very happy. He has had two successive nights of dreams. This elderly teacher is very strict with him during the online class, so much so that we use her as the scarecrow to deter him from his mischief. He says that in his dream he went to the teacher's house and she allowed him to watch cartoons throughout the day. Not only that, she gave him big buckets of chocolates, cookies, noodles and pizzas also. So he ate throughout the night. Inspired by his dream, he isn't taking her as scarecrow in real life anymore. 'Ma'am is very sweet!' he gushes.

In the second dream, a dolphin with a huge face becomes his friend. 'We play and swim together. Her mouth so big!' he says. 'She opened it and I went in for playing. We played *ludo*, me and she in her mouth. We played football also. Then we ate hot-dogs, burgers and chips. Then I came out and we played outdoors. Then we both went to what is below Leh?' he wants me to guess. 'Srinagar?' I propose. 'Yes, we went to Srinagar to enjoy.'

ᏢᏢᏢ

There are little clues lying revealingly to help us in demystification of the biggest puzzles in the scheme of nature. There is a natural art of survival without a feeling of suffering and victimization. Its protagonists are apparently subservient and soft-spoken in stark contrast to the hyperbolic obituarists who loudly shout the vainglory of struggles and mighty efforts. Like the bees in this comb.

It's harsh cold in the middle of January. It rained overnight. Everything seems beaten and surrendered to the freezing touch of the winter that is pervading around with unsettling bravery. The honeycomb has shrunk into a tight ball. There isn't a single movement to be seen. There is a wellspring of holism in being tightly around each other during testing times. The magisterial aura of holding each other tightly saves many against the onslaught of time. They weave a tapestry of courage and conviction to survive till warmer days are there.

The bees don't seem interested in shifting their positions. Those on the upper side, the front guards showing arresting quality of self-sacrifice, don't complain. It seems strictly classical. They protect those below them. They have icy dewdrops over them. The leaves are dripping with dew and mist. A few freeze to death in the line of duty. It's almost unthinkable for we humans with our fickle emotions, stupid covetousness and base pretentions to sacrifice ourselves for a larger good. There is grace, diligence and a sense of inviolable duty among the honeybees. They stand for each other. The March sun is just a month and half away. A juicy spring awaits them. Then it will be a happily buzzing place.

After being sunless for a few frozen days in January, you actually come to feel the orgasmic pleasure of the butter melting in the pan as the sun suddenly comes up and the frozen cells of your existence melt and come back to life again with the warm touch of life.

In the little clump of trees in the courtyard, a dainty oriental magpie robin retires for chilly nights. At dusk it lets out a sawing *shrrrr* call, the notes confidently full of inoffensive mischief, as if warning other birds about not barging into his home tree.

I have put a clay pitcher's neck-ring on the fence wall. It serves as a nice clay basin for putting millets for the hundreds of sparrows that roost in the nearby trees at night. They flock around with enduring versatility. Some are brooding, others are peppy. Their songs carrying myriad melodies. But they make a lot of noise while picking grains. A few bully ones chase away the docile ones, scattering the little grains on the ground. A squirrel is attracted by the din. She takes possession of the property. It sits right in the middle of the grains in the clay ring. The sparrows now show patience and sit at a distance—a picture of somberness and solemnity. Maybe they are curious to know how the squirrel uses her front paws to expertly chew the grains. A few of them hop onto the ground and pick up what they had scattered playfully. The squirrel is taking too much time. The bullying ones then start pecking at its bushy tail from behind to remind it that it has to move away.

8

A pig is genetically modified, its genes edited a bit. Its heart is then transplanted into a man. Organ harvesting will be a routine thing in future. But it would be interesting to see how the pig hearts function in our anatomy.

An Italy court has pronounced noisy toilets as human rights abuse. Well, if there is prosperity and you have well off people around then you have to eavesdrop on neighbor's toilets to have a feeling of human rights abuse.

The effects of climate change are no longer ignorable. Our technologists have a grand idea. They are planning to dim the sun by putting scattering particles in the atmosphere to reflect away the sunrays. Didn't I say sometime that we have long crossed the threshold and our hopeless solutions to our self-created problems will create still bigger problems?

ᖘᖘᖘ

The handsome dainty oriental magpie robin has picked out a particular bough for its night perch. It's suitably located among a dense clump of leaves to give it a comfortable night stay beyond the feral cats' encroachment. And the winter takes everything in its icy folds. The moon looks shivery with its beatific three-quarter smile. The winter means submission. The fast and the furious streak in us turns slower as if in proportion to the slower blood movement across veins and arteries. But then all of us know the seasons inevitably change. The spring is patiently biding its time at some virgin locales. We also have to wait and allow the cold to spend its freezing stores.

The lonely oriental magpie robin is a warm company to the forlorn writer in an old countryside house. I can feel his position. It's sad to be alone at cold nights. I believe none of us is in dumps and depression. There is hardly any sun during January. The stars twinkle sometimes at night but then the fog quickly takes possession of the skies. The smog flaunts its vile vanities—even in the countryside around the Delhi NCR. The winter air is like almost being in gas chambers but still we aren't paying any heed to the urgent climatic issues and with a flagrant indifference are adding to the concrete high-rises, spanking new complexes and thousands of new vehicles on the congested roads.

Beyond all these pressing matters, the oriental magpie robin spends his nights among a clump of *kari-patta*, guava and *parijat* branches. These intersect nicely at a safe height. The location of his favorite branch is proved by the bird-drops on the jasmine leaves below his nighttime shelter. There is a natural intelligence in creation, far bigger than our thoughts. For its nighttime homecoming, it need not look at a watch. Its coming-home time is exactly twilight, at 6:20 PM in this part. I have confirmed it a few times. It lands home exactly at twilight and breaks the eerily quiet moments with its blithely uttered *charrr-charrr* notes. It seems a kind of prayer before retiring to spend a cold night all alone and see another day.

ᏢᏢᏢ

This is something from the yellowed pages of an ancient traveler's book of life. With an unflagging persistence, he has written an indelible footnote in the book chronicling the cooing of adventurous spirits to know more of the world. It must have been astronomically breathtaking when he crossed the Himalayas and the Central Asian highlands. It's about the legendary traveler, Fahien.

More than one and half millennia ago, Fahien set out on an arduous journey. He had been ordained as a monk at a very young age. One day, he came across a very old, tattered copy of Vinay Pitika (the rules of monastic order). The sumptuous literary opulence drew his heart with its velvety cord. He wanted to have a copy of the book at any cost. Showing amazing fortitude for his age—he was already sixty-two—he set out for India, the land of the origination of his faith.

Bravely fixing the jigsaw pieces of a perilous journey, he managed to cross the Himalayas. He wandered all over India, visiting many monasteries to get the book. Finally, he found the book in Sanskrit at a monastery in Pataliputra. Sticking to his mould, he learnt Sanskrit, translated the book in his language and sailed back home. He deserved a relatively smoother sea-ride this time to go back home at the age of seventy-five.

ᕈᕈᕈ

The knowledge of a new bird species is joyful. If you are studious type, you stand on sturdier conceptual pillars. I feel more evolved and loving, at least. Great Salim Ali's book helps me a lot in this regard. It's as comprehensive on the subject as the freewheeling flights of the entire range of birds in the subcontinent. Each word carries an enriching streak. The pictures give a brilliantly crisp snapshot of the ultimate birdie reality.

Here I see a new bird on the fence wall. I take long and short notes of its colors, wings, feathers, beak and everything possible about its appearance and run to pick up the masterpiece. With a great sense of an amateur birdwatcher's emotionalism, I flip through the picture plates to spot anything matching my mental notes about the bird. Great Salim Ali will never disappoint you even if you remember a few basic points about the bird.

It turns out to be a white-browed fantail-flycatcher. It has a striking white brow. It has a distinctively white forehead and white underparts. It sometimes joins mixed hunting parties of insectivorous birds. So it possesses a pretty flexible, smart, circumstantial attitude. It flits, waltzes, pirouettes from branch to branch and tree to tree. As a tuneful tribute to the free-spirited winged birdie gods, it makes graceful sallies. Its call but is a bit harsh, a sort of authoritative *chuk-chuk*. But when it's in love it makes delightful *chee-chee-chweevi* notes. Everyone mellows down after falling in love. Well, he is always welcome in my small courtyard and little garden as long as he catches flies as suggested by his name. There are plenty of them around.

ᖘᖘᖘ

It's a reality show showcasing the taut narration of skills and talents by Godly gifted kids. With enough melody to create any lyricist's euphoria, a five-year-old girl is singing with unbelievable maturity. Every look at little Nevaan makes it plain to him that the onlooker wants him to do something in the field of 'talent'. 'It's because of the mike she holds that her voice sounds nice. The mike is very talented,' he gives his expert opinion on talent.

The talent show eggs him to do something of his own. He is all attention needed for executing something to flawless perfection. It's his sketch-work with chalk on a pillar: two human figures drawn in straight lines with an arrowed heart in between. And the elders would always comment about the kid's fancy with broken heart. By the way, the millennials are steely in nerves. They break hearts instead of being broken hearted.

He smells the prejudice, the notions of morality, etc., in my comment and changes the scenario. 'Both of them are boys,' he clarifies.

Well, two boys with a broken heart between them?

'The girl was a bad one. Both of them are crying,' he comes to the rescue of his gender.

Well, the elders might be busy in bigger struggles, leaving him as a newly born fawn struggling to its feet. But he is not a mere unsteady kitten. He has a crisp penchant for exploring newer things in his slowly growing world. Carrying a crisp vision, he has spotted a jewel on the ground. The elders, like grubby kids, are dealing with the spoilsports of the bigger world. The little researcher loiters around with inquisitive eyes. His find is something else also apart from being a jewel. It's a bug also, a jewel bug to be precise. I make him feel that it's his find, so he is very happy over the discovery. We take his find's picture and he goes around the house, showing the new species he has just discovered.

The frigid cold leaves one in need of the warmth of love and companionship more than ever. The lone jewel bug, also called metallic sheet bug, is almost frozen. They feed on plant juices. They even have the option of producing offensive odor when disturbed. The oval-shaped little shiny creature looks like a beetle, but it's a bug to be precise.

It's a brilliantly colored bug with iridescent metallic hues. Its green metallic sheen with black and red dots is surely sufficient to make Nevaan feel proud of his discovery for the benefit of the world. Its pleasantly exotic colors inspire me to Google it for more information. It comes to my knowledge that they have huge, spiky, heavily sclerotized genitalia. That makes its mating practice almost 'traumatic insemination'. It seems a marquee masculine mischief against the divinely feminine—a kind of evolutionary sexual conflict. The male bug tears through the female reproductive duct to deposit sperms, causing severe damage to the female in the process. I think all the lurid sadists out there must have a strong evolutionary memory of the jewel bugs coursing through their veins.

Maybe inspired by his discovery of a new bug species, Nevaan is adding to his clanship. His surname is Deswal. So the cats are Yellow Cat Deswal, Black Cat Deswal and the likes. So are the dogs christened along the same lines.

ᏢᏢᏢ

Those were the easy-going slow-paced days. Elegant and alluring with their nostalgic strains, still affable with their withering charm, those moments behold the enduring symbolism of goodness that shone always brighter in the past. Bathing on the well-curbs was a particularly socializing act during those times. Beyond the modern-day clanking and urging sounds, there was silence and power in those laidback moments. Time moved with a very slow, holistic elegance. It wasn't slipping away. It was in fact so plentiful that one could kill it to one's satiation. And if the bucket fell into the well, it would offer a still bigger opportunity to slaughter time en masse. A hook would be lowered at the end of a rope and many faces would calmly stare into the muddled water as the harpoon was dragged around the invisible muddy bottom. There would be just a few phrases of success in the incomprehensible paperwork of the entire set of probabilities. The rope would change many hands and it would continue for hours. A basket retrieved after dredging by many hands amounted to a very successful day in the life of all those involved including the onlookers.

ᴘᴘᴘ

A rainy sunless January forces the plants, animals and humans to crouch down in defense. The cold is both spectacular and spellbinding in its grip on our fates. The fog, smog and mists seem to be sharing an intriguing chemistry with some invisible opponent. We hardly stand any chance without Father Sun. He is the primal cause of the melodious colors of the springs that bring joy and freshness in our lives. But mother nature has profound ways of expressing her belief in life and living even among the most adverse circumstances.

As the frost-bitten leaves get withered, turn pale and tumble down, and the trees stand with bent head, and the humans stay on a low profile, one little plant has added to its fresh and greeny verve that we usually see in the monsoons. Common mallow (also called cheese mallow, cheese weed or dwarf mallow) has come of leafy youth in the depressive weather. There are lush green clumps of them by the side of countryside paths. They make the most of the wet, sunless January days. It seems they hold aloft the signature emblem of spring with their aesthetically designed leaves—palmately veined fingers branching out from the palm, circular in shape and crinkled in appearance. I expect flowers, in whitish lavender, during the spring, with purple veins.

The cold season at its peak is a testing time for the honeybees. It means survival against all odds. There are a few dozen bees that are seen sitting on the ground. They don't seem to have either energy or the spirit to fly. Why aren't they in the hive? There can be many reasons. They may be the ones that are no longer useful to the colony and thus have been expelled. It means if you aren't useful anymore, you crawl, you hardly fly anymore. These may even be the drones who just suck nectar and pollen and don't collect it. So during the winters, when there is a scarcity of resources, they get expelled from the hive. As the rest of them snug together to keep the queen alive, the idlers get paid for their uselessness. The stored honey is the lifeline through the lean season. All activity is suspended till warm spring days when the bees will set out with an exalting, energetic and enterprising spirit. In the meantime, the redundant drones are left free to devise their own ways to see through the cold. Sometimes kwing virus afflicts some of them. It deforms the wings. A bee afflicted with this malady may not have enough strength to fly back home if it commits the mistake of setting out on a cold day.

ᗺᗺᗺ

His wife may give an outraged sniff at this, and rightly so, but the simple fact is that Munsi is the number one liquor-lover in the locality as of now. 'He is of No Use!' is the public and private opinion about him. He but is not comfortable with standing out as an ungentlemanly emblem and cheekily, vehemently in fact, denies this belittling charge. Cutting through the teeth and tentacles of the not so flattering status, he elaborates through his slurred speech how he was the most *layak* among his siblings during the childhood.

They kept buffalos and the calves born in poor peasant barns had very high mortality rates because there was hardly any milk left for them. A kind of tortuous starvation it was for the little ones. With the calf gone, the buffalo ma would have problems in lactation. *Tau* Dayanand, of grand vision and pioneering conscience, had a nice solution to the problem. So even though ninety percent of their calves perished, there hardly was lactation problem among the buffalos. The process of milking ran smooth. Munsi stood, crouched rather, as the proxy calf for all the buffalo mothers grieving the loss of their kids.

A special calf robe was devised for him. Made of dark, coarse blanket, it gave him a nice calf look as he was paraded first in front of the buffalo that walloped him with slimy affection and licked him profusely. He was then made to crawl to the udder side and mock a hungriest calf's suckling at the teats. Getting to the pulsating vibrancy of motherhood, the buffalo would then get ready to fill the bucket with a magical sweetness of temper.

However, it wasn't a cakewalk all the time. In bad mood, and smelling something fishy in the business, the buffalo would sniff at him loudly, prod him playfully, even pushing with a mild punishment, which is too much for a human child. He would get kicks also sometimes as the lactation phase entered the late stage when the buffalos deny the supply of milk.

'I was the backbone of our economy during those famished days. If not for me, they would have starved to death!' he proudly elucidates his credentials that are presented to nullify the 'of no use' status bestowed upon him. He then proceeds to guzzle the remaining liquor bottle with pride.

༄༄༄

Grandfather rode his archaic Atlas cycle till his late eighties. Apparently innocuous and toothless, he had a sharp mind and still sharper willpower to hit a century of years like his favorite Sachin did on the cricket field. His classic old cycle and his frail but athletic figure presented an epic profile when you observed them slowly moving on the dusted path of life. Both seemed steeped in antiquity but you would never fail to feel the delectable charm of a pair honed by vintage years. The cycle would give panting, creaking and groaning sounds in response to his slow, easeful paddling. Maybe his joints also creaked but any sound in that genre was shadowed by his metallic companion.

I remember my first lesson in cycling at the age of twelve. With me sitting on the crossbar in front, a fodder bale at the back, Grandfather heaved the cycle at the age of eighty or a bit more. To learn cycling first you should know how to properly occupy the passenger spot anywhere possible on the cycle. That was Grandfather's advice as I tried my best to behave to the best of my capacity, juddering like an infantile passenger, trying my level best to score good marks in the art of sitting on a cycle. For a long time I was having his warning muffles above my head, 'Don't hold the handle too tight. Don't try to steer it this way or that!' Then we fell down. He plonked a hand-smash at my nape, 'Didn't I tell you not to try to steer the handle. That's the rider's job!' he exposed my grand profanity.

Three years later, we were coming in the similar manner with the slight adjustment that my still older grandpa was sitting in front as I plodded ahead with much sideways shaking of the front tyre. Grandfather forgot his own lessons in the art of being a passenger on a cycle. Not a fault of his, the frustrating cascades of my lurching paddling were sufficient to make him forget his own set of rules. No wonder, Grandfather hardly trusted my ability to see us safely home. So I found him involuntarily trying to control the handle.

It turned into a motley mix of forces in opposite directions. 'Grandpa you said it's the rider's job. Now why do you apply pressure to steer the handle?' I breathlessly protested over his headgear. 'Yea, but that's only when the rider knows to do his job properly,' he angrily countered. He followed his observation with an expert maneuver to avoid the cake-cutting ceremony of a fresh lump of dung on the way. I pulled in a different direction. The tyre cut through the dung heap as a celebratory cake-cutting of the event to follow. We were a heap of cycle, humans and the fodder bale. 'Why did you pull it while it was my job?' I complained, scared of the colossal discharge of his seasoned farmer's reflexes. 'Because you were not able to!' he shouted and feigned to smash the back of my head with his teacherly palm but stopped short, possibly realizing his role in the little accident.

After that we simply walked to our home. As a punishment, I had to pull the fodder-laden cycle, a tough job for a slightly built boy. I was sweating profusely. 'It gives a nice practice to manage the handle,' Grandfather tenderly consoled. He was slightly limping after the fall. So I was lucky not to get his favorite palm-smash at the nape. He was but luckier—in not getting a fracture after crash-landing from a cycle in his mid-eighties. So that was a close save.

ᑭᑭᑭ

Different things mean differently to various parties. There are some grains of millet. Some sparrows eat seriously;

some play and eat both; some quarrel and eat; and a few do all of this plus intimidating others. To the squirrel, it means temporary ownership of the property. It perches smartly among the grains and shoos away the sparrows. The doves don't have much use for the tiny grains but they make noise and try to stamp their docile authority. The crow has no use of it but sits in surprise as the sole owner for some time before getting bored. The doves pick a few grains from the ground among this scuffle. The cat eyes all of them as lunch items from the nearby flowerbed. It's a really hectic business. There is an understated simplicity in these tiny dollops of happenings momentarily surfacing from the ethereal vistas of the ultimate reality.

৯৯৯

My marigolds put up a brave face against harsh January to keep the banner of life and hope flying through their smiles. Now the beginning of February has better prospects for more smiles. They aren't showy and fragrant like fresh jasmine or magically alluring like dew-laden rose, but still they have enough in them to bring some traces of halcyon days among this gloomy winter. With their virtues and valor, they lit up the corner in my garden with their subdued smiles. An almost sunless January couldn't subdue their smiles. It's a world where we have decimated smiles in the wilderness across the planet. Our civilizational pursuit of El-Dorado has seen us fluently frittering away the pulsating aesthetics that mother nature had decorated along our path.

A few flowers remain, that too in the little gardens of almost obsolete people who still love flowers, who still somehow try to hold onto the majestic sinews of mother nature. Somehow wading through the broiling, intriguing corridors laid across the monochromatic hues of the modern landscape, they carry a fistful of earth and a flower smiling on that. Their rarity means they have become a treasure in their own ways.

My neighbors peep over the walls pretty greedily. This little clump of yellow, maroon and orange marigolds is drawing them like nectar-hungry drones. Any day I prefer my marigolds for the honeybees only. It's soul-pacifying sight to see the bees gathered over the table of frilled petals for a sumptuous sociality in lazy, hazy afternoons. The flowers open their hearts to the guests with an unerringly courteous smile. A month away from the spring, it seems like a thin ration line for the honeybees. But the human bumblebees want the nectar of God's blessings by offering flowers at the feet of idols in the temple. It's symbolic ritual by the way. I thing the Gods will be happier if you offer them your love and smiles and leave these few remaining flowers for the starved honeybees. Sadly, we have taken our materialistic pursuits to the extent that we won't leave any corner for them at our house.

There seems to be an impulsive scheming going around. The consumer culture is galloping by leaps and bounds with intriguing ingenuity and flawed imagination. The consumer culture is compelling, thrilling and free-flowing in its hypnotizing sway over our senses. The Godly courts are under heavy bombardment of demands by the citizens. We are always seeking more of the consumer items that would give us an edge over our neighbors. And flowers come to our mind when we set out to appease the Gods to turn the tables in our favor.

Well, my simple request to people is please forget about flowers on the altar if you don't have a place in your balcony, garden or whatever space available that can have a flowery smile. My little bed of marigolds is rapidly vanishing under the reaping tool of faith. I feel sad for the bees. Isn't it better to have lively flowers at homes—that makes them temples in themselves—instead of dead flowers at altars?

ᑭᑭᑭ

Grandfather was distinguished as a methodical peasant. As a former teacher, he carried infesting zest for studies, so education counted as his first love. He may as well could be taken as a knight in shining armor, holding his educative torch among the peasantry that was blasphemously ignorant of the importance of the books and knowledge. His love for mathematics was evocative and fulfilling. When it came to farming, he carried the same calculated, measured approach as that of a teacher.

At that time, he was an energetic man in his seventies with the withered athleticism born of a life spent in making destiny by using both mind and hands. He still managed to handle a big ox in his cart. It indeed was a huge task to keep it well behaved. By the look of it, anyone could agree that it wasn't forgettable mismatch between the bull and the owner. Grandfather would churn out intriguing novelties to keep his stamp of authority over the big beast. But despite all this, Grandpa looked a David controlling the Goliath. The beast was always well short of any adjustment and accommodation on its part to keep the cart on the track. However, the rough and rowdy beast could pull unbelievable load and that convinced its old carter to keep his faith in it. Grandfather was compelled to keep himself alert with his heightened guesswork to tame the bull's starry tantrums.

Sometimes he had to pull the rope all the way to lie flat on his back on the cart to stop the behemoth. But most often even that would be found insufficient to reign in the beast's chivalry and eccentricity born of its raw strength. On the way to the field, the bull obeyed within decent limits to Grandfather's instructions. It moved with some traces of ease, with somewhat jerky consistency. On the way back, but, the urge to eat fodder in the barn was so high that the animal would put itself on autopilot. During those moments, Grandfather looked like a helpless pilot with the machine forcing itself into autopilot mode. Grandfather's lynchings, shouts, shrieks and cuss words fell on deaf ears. However big the load to be pulled, it would run so freely as if the cart was empty. As a punishment, Grandfather would invite others to dump their fodder load on his cart but that proved ineffective as a counter measure as the cart had its load-bearing limits. The bull didn't seem in a mind to consider things in terms of the load in its cart.

Positively, it was quite decent on autopilot. It wouldn't barge into anything or anybody provided they kept a distance, so there was no serious mishap and Grandpa would ride his cart up to late seventies. After that he further went to the fields for another decade either on bicycle or hitching rides on other's carts.

During his this particular bull carting days, once he was busy picking out weed from the wheat crop. I was given the task of holding the ox's rope as it grazed on the field divides. I had the strictest instructions to hold the rope very tightly. The bull ate peacefully for fifteen minutes or so but then suddenly realized the allure of the barn fodder. I was then pulled by the rope like a little bundle of fodder.

There were just two options: either get dragged to the village or leave the rope. Thinking wise beyond my years,

I let go off the rope. Grandpa was now running behind us. He made a desperate lunge at the rope trailing behind the escaping animal. He missed it given his advanced years. I had let go off the rope and that counted as a cardinal sin in the restrictive farming religion. The bull can be pardoned because it has no concern other than eating. But me letting go off the rope smacked of gross inefficiency from human standards.

Grandpa stood aghast as the bull smartly ran away to hit its muzzle in the barn a good two kilometers away. He seemed undecided over which direction to pursue as me and the bull took to opposite directions. He thought it wise to dispense a bit of justice on the spot itself, so followed me. I would have beaten him in run any day if not for that fall in the water channel. Grandfather gave his favorite palm-swash at the back of the head—well he feigned the strike in a way so as to scare us, but in reality it severally ruffled the hair as his palm went grazing past the nape—and I ducked. He missed it. It wasn't his day that day.

Thinking wise with his mathematics-loving mind, he started slowly on the march back home, a distance of two kilometers, to get the bull back so that the cart and the fodder could be taken to the barn. I vanished into the countryside of the neighboring village. I knew exactly what to do. I postponed my arrival at the house till the arrival of Father from office at night. That was the time when Grandfather kept a low profile. True to the norms of their conflicting generations, both father and son kept a distance and muttered their dissension for each other only indirectly from a distance. A divided house serves as a chance for an opportunist like me. I silently sneaked in. Grandfather could just give cold stares at me. To rub salt on his wounds, I turned extra affectionate with Father that night, so that the last traces of taking me to justice on the next day would vanish from Grandfather's mind.

פּפּפּ

All activities are a playful game to Nevaan and everything a toy. A little heap of woolen socks nicely washed in fragrant detergent, for example. He is doodling on the wall. Childhood is always eager for a bear hug with sweet, little, innocent mischiefs. It's a dreamscape entirely in a different dimension that unfortunately we forget as we grow old, as thinking mind makes blatant transgressions into the flowering treescape of pure heart.

As he doodles, he seems one of the utmost summiteers of unbridled creativity. His lines are snaking through the established shapes and designs to chart out fresher domains on the canvas of childhood. We elders are extensive on rhetoric but puny on content. But boundless is the childhood's content. It's like riding the wave crests glowing on a full moon night. So, as he rides his shiny waves, paddling his little doodle boat with a chalk piece, he hits the shores, so needs more space to keep rowing. He needs wipers to keep enough clean space for his compelling and hypnotizing artistry. The fresh laundry serves a better purpose than what it would do in shoes. The wet woolen socks clean the walls really well.

I am jogging in the yard but my effort to still stay in workable condition is nothing more than a cat and mouse game to him. He leaves the wall clean and catches onto the piece of play offered by a middle-aged man trying to stay in shape. I am the cat so I have claws scratching my back. I am yet to overcome the shock of being a mouse then I suddenly realize I am a thief because the game has suddenly turned into police and thief. I get pounded on my modest bum as he tries to catch the thief who is trying to sneak away from the arms of law. Then he is a boxer decimating an opponent who is just shuffling around the arena. Then all and sundry games follow that he can think of on the basis of all the information he has gathered from watching cartoon programs on television.

ᎮᎮᎮ

Grandfather was named Pohker. The inspiration for the name being the Hindu month of his birth as per the lunar calendar. He was born on a date roughly falling in January, in the lunar month of *Poh*. The event must have taken place in the winters of either 1904 or 1905, he was never sure about it. Those were the times when they grew up watching and marveling at the rudimentary flying objects, the ancestors of modern planes. They called them something that would roughly come to be translated as *cheel gadis* or kite carts.

I would consider myself very lucky in one regard. I always thank God that Grandfather never played cricket in his life. There is a rigorous acceptability for hard words in peasant families. The peasants carry a heady attitude that prowls like the ramrod straight arm of the marching soldier. The addicted frenzy for rough words takes even the children in its grip. Habits are merely transferred across generations, after all. So the children in peasant families have tart tongues. Breaking the restraining ropes of etiquettes, they speak back upon their elders. With a strict guardian's rigor, the elders have still tartier fists and kicks to sum up the equation. At least that was how it was while we were growing up. And still worse during the preceding generations.

A NOBODY'S NOTEBOOK

This incident happened while I was a college-going rebel. Grandfather was considerably old at that time, in his late eighties in fact. He had a sharecropper for onions. Grandfather stocked his part of the produce in the barn, waiting for better market price. But the rains arrived before the better market conditions. The barn roof leaked. Now rottening onions will allow you to give any diabolical interpretation to the domain of bad smells. The stinking onions will eat your nerves. His preservationist plans gone haywire, he was required to sort out the rotten onions from the sound ones to protect himself from a total loss. So Grandfather needed an assistant to sort out the sellable onions from the stanching heap. I was forced into the assignment.

Rotten onions carry a swashbuckling charisma. The bad odor comes leaping and lunging to eat into your nerves and suck at the last traces of gentlemanly streak in you, if any. Grandfather, his olfactory senses dulled by the advanced years, got into the job with almost a curatorial instinct. But to me the pungent encroachment into my nostrils was darkly evocative. I kept grumbling my dissent as my hands ran through the gore of decaying onions.

I was sitting at a distance of say twelve feet from him in a corner of the barn. With a calculated familiarity with old-age born wisdom and patience, Grandfather kept his cool despite the whirlwind and spark of my igniting words of dissent. Probably he thought that even a single good, intact onion would be a nice bargain by keeping cool despite my waspish comments. He looked refreshingly restrained in this avatar.

Grandfather possessed strong-looking, lean legs and still steelier nerves. But very few good onions on one side and a big heap of rotten ones on the other, growing bigger with each passing minute, forced him to change gears in his demeanor. His hopes nosedived and temper rose. We were mired to our elbows by this time. He became aware of the enormity of his crop loss. So he did what he had postponed for so long. The cannon then burst to my igniting promptings. He hit back. He used his not so useable onions. The vollies were hurled. But his canon shots ended as monumental, metaphorical and spectacular failures. He missed all punitive attempts. Like an impish oaf I ducked, using all the experience and agility born of village games. The pulpy, squashed onions hit the wall behind me.

I can only thank God for the absence of cricket in Grandfather's life, that there was no cricket when Grandfather also played games as a boy. Otherwise, his throwing skills would have found the target to good effect. Getting a stinking squashed onion on one's face is too big a punishment for any crime. Isn't it?

ᑭᑭᑭ

The village has enough space, at least at the fringes where it melts in the farmlands, for the liquor-lovers to sit on the ground after the dark and get done with a quick wining session. The dining part would be later covered by brawls within houses and outside. Usually they take it neat and clean. Sometimes, on special occasions, they get something to eat along. The dog that we have already mentioned always howls is seen coming with a polybag in its mouth. It seems to have taken it very seriously, holds it with a serious purpose as if it will help him in beating the pangs of isolation and alienation among the groups of stray dogs.

There is something inside the bag and a single knot holds the secret. The way it trots with its grocery in its mouth, it appears that the dog is sure the contents are nothing short of gold from the standards of the canine world. It seems a little bundle of longing, joys and pathos. Our pursuits are usually centered around the little bundles that hold the source of our caprices and hallucinations tied in multiple knots in the bags. So the dog has every right to take its possession very seriously.

It looks lonely but somehow magnificent with its object. The booty holder seems to be on lookout for a suitable place to open the parcel. With extraordinary delicacy, it sneaks under a tractor trolley parked in the street. With fertile imagination and concrete capacity, it opens the single knot after a spell of dexterous pawing and mouth pulling. The first item it draws out is an empty disposable glass. The second is a plastic case for food delivery. Its lid is tight shut and inside there is some curry redolent with spicy prospects. But the little disposable tiffin's lid is beyond the water-mouthed maneuver of a dog. The retriever of this precious item is busy, giving it all in its capacity for this value-driven approach to add to the taste buds on its tongue. Meanwhile, a female dog comes stealthily from behind. Nicely gets into position and pees with meditative effortlessness on the canine shopper's shopping bag. Some of her friends, looking hard-nosed and thoughtful, curiously stare from a distance.

His shopping vandalized, the offended shopper whines angrily, gives a spurt of howl and runs after her to teach her a lesson. Her friends then escape with the provisions to play with it and scatter the contents in the street to add to their part in the chaos around.

ᐁᐁᐁ

The spring is always waiting in the wings; like a spiky creeper looping around her cold lover. Basant Panchami, falling on February 5 this year, amounts to sowing the spring seeds that would blossom smiles in March. It's the start of sunnier days with a balmy tonality. The seasons have an amazing, tactical flexibility that allows healthy transitions and undisputed takeovers.

The festive occasion is but a kind of setback for the honeybees. They have been brave and tried to undo the limiting definitions of inclement weather to survive for sunnier days. Sadly, their nice round hive is attacked by the honey buzzard. His beak pecks with a notational intent. The hive gets misshapen as he steals away their precious store of honey. I watch from a distance. I can feel that something is missing. Dry leaves tumble down because the big predator' wings ruffle the branches. We humans suffer the flatness of our sweeping conclusions. To my analytical wit, the eagle is an unsober and hostile bird. My reality is that the bees are buzzing in the air with a sense of loss. But maybe their truth is something very different from my feeling.

The eagle flutters away with a shrieking note. From my linear perspective, the hive seems like an amoeba now. But then my human-born pain withers away and some unconditional truth lands in my senses like a lyrical oasis. There is always a balance in nature. Still there is something left to build the house again, to make a new beginning. There is surely some reserve to last for some more days. They just need their queen to be safe for a riveting fresh start in the spring. The rest they will undoubtedly manage, especially now when we have the February sun smiling kindly. The spring will unfold its subtle coils and will unleash many flowery smiles.

Unlike we humans they don't complain and waste their energy in the blame game. They have a vaulting clarity in their 'being' in contrast to our efforts at 'becoming' with our limpid ambitions. Within half an hour, the tattered house is far better in appearance. It's not smooth and round like earlier. There are irregular edges as the bees work back to their former positions. The eagle is but still circling in the air. I'm sure it has taken enough for one square meal. There are so few eagles left and a small number of beehives. Looking at such little survival games, it appears as if all isn't lost. It's a bit assuring.

ᗞᗞᗞ

An asian pied starling is carrying a few feet long thin strip of light fabric in its beak as it flies to its construction site. It's a busy world engaged in making, breaking and remaking. She has an equal right to make something as anyone around. The tiny tailorbird plays mischief and takes a snipe at the lower end. The big group of house sparrows raises a laughing chorus. A brahmani mynah shrieks with delight. A peacock looks eagerly with the stately extravagance of its colors. A squirrel scuttles around with a kind of gestural vocabulary. On a neighbor's wall an alpha male monkey moves with a haughty demeanor. Looking at him, I realize we carry a pretty hoary ancestry.

The honey buzzard hasn't yet forgotten about its honeyed lunch. It's circling above in the sky, maybe staring at me accusatively as I sit on a chair in the courtyard near the tree bearing the hive. I intend to write something here, but then he doesn't know that it's only a struggling countryside writer. He supposes that the honeybees have summoned my services to scare him. I'm thankful to him that he is scared because if he attacks I'll run sooner than the honeybees.

There is an eerie stillness after the ripples of birdie noise let loose by the tiny tailorbird's adventure. The little garden around me seems capable of maintaining a sustainable and dynamic paradigm. I sit with a retrospective aura, a kind of thin-veiled misty cloud around me born of engaging self-reflectivity. All of us possess multilayered individual histories shaped by the sharp edges of irony hitting at our existence with a kind of gentle madness. A gentle breeze blows with its suggestive touches at the leaves of the trees.

ᐯᐯᐯ

Nevaan's words during the online classes are highly censored. A little soul's words of innocence can expose mountains of elderly hypocrisies. Childhood innocence is startingly stylized for truth. It comes from a resounding depth of purity sustained by an unconditioned and uncustomized self.

One day he is given freedom to give his uncensored speech on the topic of mother. It falls with the force of classical weight on feathery modernity. 'Mama is very good. She does all my homework. She gets very angry also and sometimes pulls my hair,' his rare repertoire of praising words leaves his mother teary eyed. 'I devote my entire day for his welfare and look what I get in return,' she is inconsolable. But then she has realized that he is free in his opinions and is swimming with powerful frog-kicks in the pool of childhood independence.

So now he has to do his own homework. His mother has said a firm *no* to do it for him after his sting operation. He is asked to 'write five lines on Nevaan'. He is seen very busy for twenty minutes with the below given essay in the middle of the page:

'Write five lines on Nevaan. He doesn't like reading and writing. He wants to play all the time. He wants to watch cartoon TV all the time. He wants a roomful of chips.'

That marks his little summary of paradise. This candid and instamatic write-up brings more tears in the eyes of his mother. With a lyrical fluency, Nevaan is sauntering around to do full justice to his essay.

He is seen standing in front of Labrador Tuffy, the friendly pet from the neighborhood. Labrador Tuffy barks in a friendly tone. 'How are you Tuffy?' he asks. The dog wags its tail and replies in soft friendly barkings. Nevaan also starts doing *bho-bho* in varied tones. The conversation goes for about fifteen minutes. An objection is raised against Nevaan's barking. 'But we are talking in his language. I tried and thought he would reply in our language. But seems he cannot do it, so I changed my language to talk to him in his own,' he replies in a prescriptive tone.

ᖰᖰᖰ

This peacock has a hand-length of plumage. It looks quite handsome with it, something of rugged little stubble charm of masculinity. Full fantail is cumbersome. It keeps it tethered to the centricity of amorous passion, making it a love-haunted soul. It also means a lot of effort while flying, almost bum-busting effort. And the total absence of plumage also gives too much of a clean-shaven look to a peacock. But with this short plumage, it looks dapper smart and can fly to its satisfaction.

The red-vented bulbul is seen after two-three months. I believe it had gone visiting some relative. Maybe got bored with the uneventfulness of life here. Now it looks fresh with profound and impressionistic attitude.

A cat got onto the *neem* tree. The cat has no business there. So a crow, a couple of mynas, three-four pied starlings and some babblers raise such a din that it has to jump off the tree. The compendium of birdie platitudes starts a little chain of repercussions. The intimidating squirrel, which has grabbed the millet bowl all for itself after shooing away the sparrows, now runs away trippingly. It thinks the cat has jumped with a decisive attempt at its life. The fresh-from-journey bulbul gives it a nice chase over the wall top. The sparrows shout in merriment.

Printed in the USA
CPSIA information can be obtained
at www.ICGtesting.com
LVHW041230051023
760079LV00002B/442